Faith Over Fear: 50 Scriptures to Calm Your Mind and Renew Your Spirit

Willie London II

Published by Willie London II, 2024.

FAITH OVER FEAR: 50 SCRIPTURES TO CALM YOUR MIND AND RENEW YOUR SPIRIT

First edition. December 22, 2024.

ISBN: 979-8230023340

Written by Willie London II.

Table of Contents

Introduction

Finding Rest in a Restless World

Stress and anxiety have become universal struggles in today's fast-paced world. Whether you're balancing work, family, health, or personal challenges, life's demands can often feel overwhelming. But what if the solution wasn't about doing more, but trusting more? What if peace wasn't about finding the perfect circumstances but discovering the perfect love of Christ?

Faith Over Fear is a journey through 50 powerful scriptures, each offering practical guidance and spiritual encouragement for overcoming life's challenges. These chapters are designed to help you shift your focus from the chaos around you to the peace within you—peace that only comes from a deep relationship with God.

Through this book, you'll learn how to:

- Find strength in your weaknesses.
- Trust God's promises, even in uncertainty.
- Experience His peace that transcends all understanding.
- Walk in faith, knowing that He is with you every step of the way.

This isn't just a book about stress management; it's about transformation. It's about discovering the self-love that comes from seeing yourself as God sees you—fully known, fully loved, and fully equipped to navigate life's challenges. My prayer is that each chapter will draw you closer to Christ, helping you to live with the confidence, peace, and joy He desires for you.

So, take a deep breath, open your heart, and let's embark on this journey together.

Chapter 1: Peace Through Prayer (Philippians 4:6-7)

Verse:

"Do not be anxious about anything, but in every situation, by prayer and petition, with thanksgiving, present your requests to God. And the peace of God, which transcends all understanding, will guard your hearts and your minds in Christ Jesus."

Anxiety can feel like an inescapable weight—constant, relentless, and draining. It clouds our minds with fear, robs us of peace, and keeps us trapped in cycles of worry. In Philippians 4:6-7, Paul offers a profound antidote: prayer. This verse provides a practical and spiritual roadmap for managing anxiety, encouraging us to shift our focus from fear to faith.

Paul's words are not just comforting; they're revolutionary. The command to "be anxious about nothing" challenges our natural tendencies to overthink and hold onto control. Instead, Paul invites us to bring every concern—big or small—before God. Through prayer and thanksgiving, we're not simply asking for solutions; we're surrendering our need to manage everything on our own. This act of release is the first step toward experiencing the supernatural peace that only God can provide.

Why Prayer Calms Anxiety

Prayer is not a passive act; it's a deliberate choice to trust God. When we pray, we shift the burden of control from ourselves to the One who is fully capable of handling it. Anxiety often stems from trying to manage things beyond our ability to control. Prayer interrupts that cycle, reminding us that God is in charge, not us.

Paul emphasizes that this peace "transcends all understanding." In other words, it's not logical or tied to our circumstances. You might still be facing uncertainty or difficulty, but through prayer, God's peace becomes a fortress around your heart and mind. This peace is not about avoiding problems—it's about knowing that God walks with you through them.

The Power of Gratitude in Prayer

Paul's instruction to pray with thanksgiving is a key element of this verse. Why gratitude? Because gratitude shifts our perspective from what's missing to what's present. When we thank God, even in challenging situations, we anchor ourselves in His goodness and faithfulness. Gratitude reminds us of all the ways He has already provided, giving us confidence that He will do so again.

Scientific studies align with this biblical wisdom. Research shows that practicing gratitude lowers stress, reduces anxiety, and promotes emotional resilience. Gratitude isn't just about being polite—it rewires the brain, helping us focus on the positive rather than the overwhelming. When paired with prayer, thanksgiving becomes a powerful tool to combat the grip of anxiety.

Practical Ways to Apply Philippians 4:6-7

Here are practical steps to incorporate prayer and gratitude into your daily life to manage anxiety:

1. **Pray Specifically:** When anxiety arises, don't just say, "Help me, Lord." Be specific about what's troubling you. Present your concerns clearly to God, trusting Him with the details.
2. **Start and End with Gratitude:** Begin your prayers by

thanking God for His past faithfulness and end by expressing trust in His plans. Gratitude bookends your prayers with hope.

3. **Memorize and Meditate on the Verse:** Use Philippians 4:6-7 as a mental anchor. Repeat it whenever worry starts to creep in. Let it become a shield for your heart and mind.
4. **Write a Prayer Journal:** Record your fears, prayers, and moments of thanksgiving. Over time, revisit how God has answered those prayers to strengthen your trust in Him.

God's Peace in Action

The peace Paul describes in Philippians 4:7 is not a fleeting feeling but a divine assurance that God is in control. Think back to a time when you faced uncertainty or difficulty yet experienced an unexplainable calm. That's the peace Paul is referencing—a peace that doesn't make sense to the human mind because it comes from God, not from circumstances.

This peace guards your heart, protecting it from the relentless pull of fear, and it guards your mind, helping you focus on the truth instead of spiraling into worry. Prayer, when paired with thanksgiving, unlocks this peace and equips you to navigate life's challenges with confidence.

An Invitation to Trust

Philippians 4:6-7 is more than a command—it's an invitation. Anxiety tells us to hold on tighter, to manage and control every detail. But this verse tells us to do the opposite: release it. When you bring your fears to God in prayer and pair them with gratitude, you are declaring, "I trust You."

What are you holding onto that God is asking you to release? Take a moment to name it, write it down, and bring it before Him in prayer.

Trust that the peace He promises will follow—a peace that guards your heart and mind, no matter what lies ahead.

Chapter 2: Living in the Present (Matthew 6:34)

Verse:

"Therefore do not worry about tomorrow, for tomorrow will worry about itself. Each day has enough trouble of its own."

Anxiety often pulls us out of the present moment. It drags our minds to the endless "what-ifs" of tomorrow, planting seeds of fear and doubt about things that haven't even happened yet. In Matthew 6:34, Jesus offers a practical piece of wisdom that is as relevant today as it was 2,000 years ago: stay present. He reminds us that while tomorrow may bring its own challenges, it is not ours to control or fear today.

This verse doesn't dismiss the reality of planning or preparation. Instead, it speaks directly to the habit of worrying about things beyond our control. Worry doesn't equip us for tomorrow—it robs us of the strength we need today. Living in the present is not just a nice idea; it is a command from Jesus Himself, one that frees us to trust God fully with our future.

When we focus on today, we begin to see the beauty and opportunities that God has placed in front of us. Worry blinds us to these blessings. It keeps us from fully appreciating the relationships, moments, and resources we have right now. Jesus is inviting us to release our need to know every detail of what's coming next and instead trust that He will provide for tomorrow, just as He is providing for today.

The Role of Trust in Managing Anxiety

At its core, worry is rooted in a lack of trust. We feel the need to anticipate and control the future because we don't fully believe that things will work out without our intervention. Matthew 6:34 challenges us to let go of that mindset. Trusting God with our tomorrow doesn't mean ignoring responsibilities—it means recognizing that His plans are greater than our fears.

Imagine this: You're carrying a heavy backpack filled with rocks, each one representing a worry about tomorrow. As you walk, the weight slows you down and exhausts you. Jesus is saying, "Put the backpack down. You don't need to carry that load." Trusting Him means handing over the rocks, one by one, and walking forward unburdened.

Practical Ways to Stay Present

1. **Practice Mindfulness in Prayer:**
   When anxiety about the future creeps in, take a few moments to pray and intentionally focus on the present. Start by thanking God for the blessings of today—your health, the air you're breathing, the meal you just ate. Ask Him to help you trust Him with what lies ahead. This small practice can re-center your thoughts and bring you back to the moment.
2. **Focus on What You Can Do Today:**
   Break your day into manageable pieces. Instead of thinking about the entire week or month, ask yourself, "What can I do right now to honor God and reduce stress?" Maybe it's completing one task on your list, having a meaningful conversation, or simply taking a moment to breathe deeply.
3. **Embrace Gratitude as a Daily Habit:**
   Keeping a gratitude journal can ground you in the present. Each day, write down three things you are thankful for. They don't have to be monumental—small blessings like a kind word from a friend or the sound of birds outside your

window can remind you that today has its own joys.

4. **Limit Overplanning:**
   While it's wise to plan, overplanning can feed anxiety. Set aside specific times to plan and organize, but don't dwell on it all day. Once your plan is set, trust God with the outcome.

Living in Today's Strength

There's a reason Jesus emphasizes focusing on today: God's grace is sufficient for the moment we're in, not the ones we've imagined in the future. When we stretch ourselves to cover tomorrow's challenges prematurely, we run out of strength. But when we trust Him for today, we find that His grace is perfectly proportioned to our needs.

Consider the Israelites in the wilderness. God provided manna each morning, just enough for that day. If they tried to hoard it, the manna spoiled. This was God's way of teaching them to depend on Him daily, not just for provision but for trust. The same principle applies to our anxieties about the future: God will provide for tomorrow, but He calls us to trust Him one day at a time.

The Science of Presence

Psychologically, staying present can drastically reduce anxiety. Research shows that mindfulness—fully engaging in the present moment—lowers cortisol levels and improves mental clarity. Dwelling on the future often activates the brain's stress response, keeping us in a constant state of fight or flight. Practicing presence, on the other hand, helps the mind to rest.

An Invitation to Trust

Jesus is not asking us to ignore our responsibilities or pretend life is easy. He knows that each day has its own challenges. But He is inviting us to trust Him more deeply. What if you could face each day with confidence, knowing that you don't have to tackle tomorrow's problems until tomorrow? That freedom is available to you when you trust God with your future.

As you reflect on Matthew 6:34, ask yourself: What am I holding onto that belongs to tomorrow? Write it down, and then take a moment to pray, releasing it to God. Trust Him with your backpack of worries, and embrace the peace that comes from living in the present.

Chapter 3: God Hears Your Distress (Psalm 34:17)

Verse:

"The righteous cry out, and the Lord hears them; he delivers them from all their troubles."

Stress often creates a sense of isolation, a belief that no one truly understands the weight we're carrying. In the silence of our struggles, the enemy plants seeds of doubt, whispering, "You're alone in this." But Psalm 34:17 counters that lie with a profound truth: when the righteous cry out, God hears. Not only does He hear, but He also delivers. His ear is tuned to the cries of His children, and His heart moves to act on their behalf.

This verse reminds us that crying out to God is not a sign of weakness but a declaration of faith. It acknowledges our dependence on Him and invites His strength into our lives. When we turn to God in times of trouble, we're not just venting our frustrations—we're aligning ourselves with His power to overcome.

Many people struggle with asking for help, believing it's a sign of failure or inadequacy. But God doesn't see it that way. When we cry out to Him, we're not exposing weakness—we're demonstrating trust. Imagine a child calling out to their parent for comfort or safety. That cry is a reflection of the bond between them. In the same way, crying out to God reveals the depth of our relationship with Him. It's an act of surrender, recognizing that He is the only one who can truly deliver us.

Stress and anxiety often tempt us to withdraw, to keep our struggles bottled up inside. But God calls us to do the opposite: to vocalize our pain, to articulate our fears, and to bring them to Him. He invites us to share every detail of our troubles, no matter how small or overwhelming they may seem.

Psalm 34:17 goes beyond reassurance—it is a promise. When the righteous cry out, God not only hears but also delivers. His response may not always look the way we expect, but it is always perfect. Sometimes deliverance comes as a solution to the problem; other times, it's the strength to endure. Either way, His presence brings peace in the midst of chaos.

Consider how God delivered David, the writer of this psalm, from countless dangers. Whether fleeing from King Saul or facing external threats, David experienced God's protection repeatedly. His life was a testament to the truth of this verse: God hears and acts. Even when deliverance wasn't immediate, David trusted that God was at work behind the scenes.

Prayer doesn't have to be formal or structured. In moments of stress, speak to God as you would to a trusted friend. Let the words flow naturally, expressing exactly how you feel. You don't need to filter your emotions—God already knows your heart. Writing down your struggles can also be a powerful way to cry out to God. As you journal, invite Him into your thoughts. End each entry by asking for His guidance and deliverance, trusting that He will respond. Music, too, can connect us to God in profound ways. Choose worship songs that reflect your feelings and sing them as a form of prayer, surrendering your worries through song.

While crying out to God is vital, He often works through others to bring deliverance. Share your burdens with trusted friends, family members, or a mentor who can pray with you and provide encouragement. God designed us for community, and He often uses others to remind us of His presence and care.

Research shows that expressing emotions reduces stress. When we verbalize our struggles, our brain releases chemicals that promote emotional regulation. Crying out to God takes this a step further, combining the psychological benefits of expression with the spiritual comfort of knowing we are heard by a loving Creator. It is both an emotional release and an act of faith, creating space for God to work in our lives.

A young man overwhelmed by financial pressures cried out to God one night, pouring out his frustrations and fears. The next day, an unexpected job opportunity arose—a direct answer to his prayer. While not every cry is met with such immediate resolution, this story illustrates how God moves when we surrender our troubles to Him. It's important to remember, however, that God's timing is not always our own. While we may want instant relief, His plan often involves growth and preparation. Waiting can be difficult, but it is in these moments that our faith is strengthened. Even when deliverance seems delayed, we can trust that God is working all things for our good.

As you meditate on this verse, consider the areas of your life where you need to cry out to God. What burdens have you been carrying in silence? Take a moment to voice them, either through prayer, journaling, or even a quiet thought directed toward Him. Trust that He hears you and is already at work bringing deliverance.

Psalm 34:17 invites us to live with the confidence that we are never alone in our struggles. God hears every cry, and His response is rooted in love. The next time stress threatens to overwhelm you, remember this promise: the Creator of the universe is listening, and He will deliver you.

Chapter 4: God's Presence in Fear (Isaiah 41:10)

Verse:

"So do not fear, for I am with you; do not be dismayed, for I am your God. I will strengthen you and help you; I will uphold you with my righteous right hand."

Fear is a powerful emotion. It has the ability to paralyze, distort reality, and leave us feeling vulnerable and helpless. Isaiah 41:10 addresses fear directly, offering not only comfort but also an unshakable assurance: God is with us. This verse is a reminder that while fear may come, it does not have to consume us, because we are not facing it alone.

The words "do not fear" and "do not be dismayed" are not casual suggestions—they are commands from a loving Father. God's presence in our lives is the antidote to fear. He doesn't dismiss our feelings but instead replaces them with His strength, help, and sustaining power. This verse gives us four promises: His presence ("I am with you"), His reassurance ("do not be dismayed"), His strength ("I will strengthen you"), and His support ("I will uphold you").

The Paralyzing Nature of Fear

Fear often thrives in uncertainty. It grows in the shadows of the unknown, convincing us that danger lurks around every corner. This can manifest in stress about the future, anxiety over relationships, or worry about failure. When fear takes root, it can prevent us from stepping forward into opportunities God has placed before us. Isaiah 41:10 confronts this head-on by reminding us that we don't have to rely on our own strength. God's power and presence are always greater than the forces that intimidate us.

Fear also loves isolation. It tells us we're alone in our struggles and that no one understands. But this verse is a direct contradiction to that lie. "I am with you" is a declaration that God is always by our side, even in the darkest moments. His companionship is not conditional or fleeting; it is steadfast and unchanging.

Living in Courage Through God's Strength

Courage is not the absence of fear but the ability to move forward despite it. When we rely on God, we gain a courage that is not rooted in our abilities but in His promises. Isaiah 41:10 reminds us that His strength is available to us. He doesn't just offer abstract encouragement; He offers real, sustaining power that enables us to face challenges head-on.

Imagine a child learning to ride a bike. At first, they're terrified of falling, but when a parent runs alongside, holding them steady, the fear begins to fade. God's presence in our lives is much like that parent's steadying hand. He doesn't promise a life free of falls, but He does promise to uphold us and help us rise again.

Practical Steps to Overcome Fear

1. **Anchor Yourself in God's Word**
   When fear arises, turn to scripture. Meditate on verses like Isaiah 41:10, repeating them aloud if necessary. Let the truth of God's promises drown out the lies of fear.
2. **Pray for Strength and Guidance**
   Instead of focusing on what you can't control, bring your fears to God in prayer. Ask for His strength to face the situation and His guidance to navigate it.

3. **Challenge Negative Thoughts**
   Fear often stems from worst-case scenarios we imagine in our minds. Combat this by asking yourself, "What evidence do I have that this will happen?" Then, remind yourself of God's faithfulness in past challenges.
4. **Take Action in Small Steps**
   Fear often diminishes when we take practical steps forward. Break your challenge into smaller tasks and ask God to help you tackle each one with courage.

The Role of Faith in Fear

Faith and fear cannot coexist. When we choose faith, we actively reject the hold fear has over us. Faith reminds us that God is in control, even when life feels uncertain. Trusting Him doesn't mean we'll never feel afraid, but it does mean that fear won't define our actions. It shifts our focus from what could go wrong to what God can do.

A Real-Life Story of Courage

A single mother facing eviction once shared how she clung to Isaiah 41:10 during her darkest days. She had no idea where she and her children would live, but she chose to pray daily, asking God for strength and guidance. Within weeks, she received unexpected help from a community organization, providing her with housing and resources. Her faith in God's presence gave her the courage to keep going, even when the future seemed bleak.

Reflection on Isaiah 41:10

Take a moment to reflect on the fears that have been holding you back. Write them down and place them next to this verse. Ask yourself, "What would my life look like if I truly believed God was with me in this?" Then pray, surrendering your fears to Him and inviting His strength into your life.

Walking Forward Without Fear

Fear may come knocking, but you don't have to answer the door. With God's presence, you can face life's challenges with confidence and peace. His promise to strengthen, help, and uphold you is unchanging. The next time fear creeps in, remember Isaiah 41:10 and step forward in faith, knowing that you are never alone.

Chapter 5: Christ's Peace (John 14:27)

Verse:

"Peace I leave with you; my peace I give you. I do not give to you as the world gives. Do not let your hearts be troubled and do not be afraid."

In a world filled with noise, uncertainty, and constant demands, peace can feel like a fleeting dream. We often equate peace with a lack of conflict or difficulty, believing it can only exist when everything is calm and in order. But in John 14:27, Jesus offers us a radically different kind of peace—a peace that transcends circumstances and quiets the soul even in the midst of chaos.

This verse is part of Jesus' farewell discourse to His disciples. Knowing they would soon face trials, betrayals, and His death, He spoke these words to comfort and prepare them. The peace Jesus offers is not like the temporary comfort the world provides, which is often rooted in distractions or material security. Instead, His peace is enduring and unshakable, anchored in the presence of God.

What Makes Christ's Peace Different?

The world offers peace in fragments: a relaxing vacation, a few moments of silence, or temporary solutions to problems. These forms of peace are dependent on external factors and often disappear as quickly as they arrive. In contrast, Christ's peace is internal and eternal. It is not tied to what's happening around us but to who He is. When we accept His peace, it becomes a shield for our hearts, guarding us against the turmoil that life inevitably brings.

Jesus emphasizes this by saying, "Do not let your hearts be troubled and do not be afraid." This is not a denial of life's challenges but a reminder that we don't have to face them alone. His peace is a gift, freely given, and it equips us to rise above fear and anxiety.

How Do We Receive This Peace?

Receiving Christ's peace requires a conscious decision to trust Him. It begins with surrender—letting go of the need to control every outcome and placing our faith in His sovereignty. When we release our grip on worry and allow Him to take the lead, His peace begins to fill the spaces where fear once lived.

This peace also grows through relationship. Spending time with Jesus in prayer, reading scripture, and meditating on His promises deepens our awareness of His presence. The more we align our hearts with His, the more His peace becomes a natural part of our lives.

Practical Steps to Embrace Christ's Peace

1. **Create a Daily Quiet Time:**
   Dedicate a portion of your day to be still before God. Use this time to reflect on His promises, pray, and listen for His guidance. This practice helps center your mind and invites His peace into your day.
2. **Turn to Him in the Moment:**
   When anxiety or stress arises, pause and pray. Simply saying, "Jesus, I trust you," can redirect your focus and calm your spirit.
3. **Memorize Scriptures on Peace:**
   Verses like John 14:27 can serve as anchors during difficult times. Repeating them aloud or in your mind can remind you of His presence and promises.
4. **Limit External Noise:**

Reduce distractions that contribute to stress, such as excessive news consumption or social media. Fill that time with worship music, scripture reading, or moments of quiet reflection.

The Transformative Power of Peace

Christ's peace doesn't mean we will never experience stress or fear. Instead, it transforms how we respond to those feelings. When we carry His peace, we can face challenges with a calm assurance that God is in control. This peace enables us to make decisions with clarity, maintain healthy relationships, and persevere through trials without becoming overwhelmed.

A Testimony of Peace

A woman facing a terminal illness shared how John 14:27 became her lifeline. Despite the grim diagnosis, she chose to focus on Jesus' promise of peace. Through prayer and meditation on His words, she found an inner calm that defied her circumstances. Her testimony inspired those around her, showing that Christ's peace is not just a concept but a tangible reality.

Reflection on John 14:27

Take a moment to reflect on the areas of your life where peace feels absent. What worries or fears are troubling your heart? Write them down, and beside each one, write Jesus' words: "My peace I give you." Pray over this list, asking Him to replace your anxiety with His peace.

Walking in Peace

Jesus' peace is not a fleeting promise—it is a gift meant to sustain you every day. As you face the stresses and uncertainties of life, let this verse remind you that His peace is yours to claim. Do not let your heart be troubled. Instead, rest in the knowledge that His peace is with you, guarding your heart and mind in every situation.

Chapter 6: Relinquishing Burdens (Psalm 55:22)

Verse:

"Cast your cares on the Lord and he will sustain you; he will never let the righteous be shaken."

Stress often feels like carrying an invisible weight. It pulls on your mind, drains your energy, and makes every step feel heavier. Psalm 55:22 offers a solution to this exhausting cycle: cast your cares on the Lord. This verse doesn't suggest that we ignore or suppress our worries—it invites us to release them to the One who can truly handle them.

The word "cast" is intentional. It implies an active decision to throw off burdens rather than holding onto them. It's a picture of trust, a moment where we say, "Lord, I can't carry this anymore, but I know You can." And God promises not only to sustain us but also to ensure that we remain unshaken, even in life's storms.

The Struggle to Let Go

Letting go of burdens can feel unnatural. We're conditioned to solve our problems, to figure things out on our own. But this self-reliance often leads to burnout and frustration. Psalm 55:22 challenges us to break that pattern. Instead of trying to control everything, we're called to trust in God's sustaining power.

This trust doesn't mean that our problems will disappear instantly. Sometimes, casting our cares on the Lord is a daily, even moment-by-moment decision. But with each surrender, we experience His peace and strength in new ways.

God's Role as Sustainer

The promise in this verse is twofold: God will sustain you, and He will not allow the righteous to be shaken. To sustain means to uphold, to provide the strength needed to endure. When life feels overwhelming, God steps in to carry what we cannot. He doesn't promise a burden-free life, but He does promise that we will never face those burdens alone.

Practical Ways to Cast Your Cares

1. **Name Your Burdens**
   Take time to identify what's weighing on you. Whether it's financial stress, relational conflict, or health concerns, naming your burdens can make them feel more manageable. Once identified, bring each one to God in prayer.
2. **Visualize Surrender**
   Imagine physically handing your worries to God. Close your eyes and picture placing each burden into His hands. This exercise can help solidify your trust in His ability to carry them.
3. **Replace Worry with Prayer**
   Each time a worry arises, turn it into a prayer. Instead of dwelling on what could go wrong, focus on God's promises. Use this verse as a reminder: "Lord, I cast this care onto You. Sustain me and keep me unshaken."
4. **Seek Support**
   God often works through people to help lighten our loads. Don't hesitate to share your struggles with a trusted friend, mentor, or counselor. They can offer prayer, guidance, and encouragement.

The Strength Found in Surrender

Releasing your burdens to God doesn't mean giving up—it means recognizing your limitations and leaning on His limitless strength. When you cast your cares on Him, you make room for His power to work in your life. This surrender frees you from the mental and emotional exhaustion of trying to do everything on your own.

Consider Jesus' words in Matthew 11:28-30: "Come to me, all you who are weary and burdened, and I will give you rest." God's desire is not for you to struggle under the weight of stress but to find rest in His presence. By casting your cares on Him, you step into the rest and renewal He promises.

A Real-Life Illustration

A man struggling with a failing business felt the crushing weight of financial stress. Every night, he lay awake, running through scenarios and trying to find solutions. One evening, he prayed Psalm 55:22 aloud, surrendering his worries to God. Over time, he began to experience a sense of peace and clarity. Though his circumstances didn't change immediately, his perspective did. He started to see opportunities where he once saw obstacles, trusting that God was sustaining him through the process.

Reflection on Psalm 55:22

Think about the burdens you're carrying today. Write them down, one by one, and place them beside this verse. Then pray, "Lord, I cast these cares onto You. Sustain me as I walk through this season. Help me trust in Your promise that I will not be shaken."

Walking Forward Without the Weight

Life's challenges may not disappear, but when you cast your cares on the Lord, the weight of those challenges shifts. Instead of carrying them alone, you walk with the assurance that God is carrying them with you.

Trust in His sustaining power, and let Psalm 55:22 remind you that you are never alone in your struggles.

Chapter 7: Relinquishing Anxiety to God's Care (1 Peter 5:7)

Verse:

"Cast all your anxiety on him because he cares for you."

Anxiety is an unwelcome companion that whispers lies into your mind—lies that you are not enough, that the future is uncertain, and that you are alone in facing life's challenges. But 1 Peter 5:7 offers a profound and liberating truth: you are not meant to carry anxiety by yourself. This verse reminds us that God not only sees our struggles but deeply cares about them. He invites us to cast all our anxiety onto Him because He is invested in our well-being.

The word "cast" conveys a sense of urgency and decisiveness. It's not a timid or partial action but a full and deliberate surrender. God's care for us is not passive or distant; it is active and personal. He longs to replace the weight of anxiety with His peace, but first, we must take the step of giving our worries to Him.

God's Care: A Foundation for Trust

It's one thing to know that God is powerful, but it's another to believe that He cares about the details of your life. Many people struggle with this concept, feeling as though their concerns are too small or insignificant to bring to God. However, this verse dismantles that misconception. If something is weighing on your heart, it matters to God. His care is not limited by size or scope. He cares for the grand moments of your life and the quiet fears that keep you awake at night.

God's care is also consistent. Unlike the fleeting attention we might receive from others, His care is unchanging and eternal. When we cast our anxiety on Him, we are placing it in the hands of the One who is fully capable of handling it and fully committed to us.

The Weight of Anxiety

Anxiety often feels like a heavy load strapped to your back. It slows your progress, saps your energy, and clouds your perspective. Carrying it alone can lead to burnout, physical illness, and emotional exhaustion. This verse offers a radical alternative: instead of bearing the weight, give it to the One who can carry it for you. Casting your anxiety on God doesn't mean ignoring it or pretending it doesn't exist; it means choosing to trust Him with it.

Practical Ways to Cast Anxiety on God

1. **Identify Your Triggers:**
   Take time to reflect on what causes your anxiety. Is it fear of failure, uncertainty about the future, or the opinions of others? Naming these triggers can help you approach them intentionally in prayer.
2. **Create a Surrender Journal:**
   Write down your worries and physically "hand them over" to God by closing the journal after each entry. This symbolic act can help you internalize the idea of letting go.
3. **Practice Breath Prayers:**
   Use short, repetitive prayers that align with this verse, such as "Lord, I cast my cares on You." Combine this with deep breathing to calm your mind and body.
4. **Seek Support in the Community:**
   Share your struggles with a trusted friend, mentor, or church leader who can pray with you and remind you of God's care. Sometimes, hearing God's promises from another person can

strengthen your faith.

God's Promises in Exchange for Anxiety

When we cast our anxiety on God, He doesn't leave us empty-handed. In return, He offers His peace, presence, and guidance. Philippians 4:6-7 reinforces this: when we bring our concerns to God in prayer, His peace guards our hearts and minds. This peace is not dependent on circumstances; it flows from the assurance that God is in control.

A Story of Casting Anxiety

A young woman facing a high-pressure exam felt overwhelmed by the fear of failure. She couldn't sleep or focus, and the anxiety began to affect her health. One night, she knelt in prayer and fully surrendered her fears to God, repeating 1 Peter 5:7 aloud. The next morning, she experienced an unexpected sense of calm. Although the exam was challenging, she found the clarity and focus to do her best. She later realized that God's care wasn't just about the outcome but about sustaining her through the process.

Reflection on 1 Peter 5:7

What anxieties are you holding onto today? Take a moment to name them, either in your mind or on paper. As you reflect on this verse, picture yourself handing each one to God. Pray, "Lord, I cast my anxieties on You. Help me trust in Your care and rely on Your strength."

Living in Freedom from Anxiety

Anxiety doesn't have to define your life. With each worry you release to God, you take a step toward freedom. Remember, God's care for you is deep, personal, and unwavering. Let 1 Peter 5:7 be a reminder that you are never alone in your struggles. Cast your anxiety on Him, and walk forward in the peace and confidence that comes from knowing He is always with you.

Chapter 8: Trust in God's Guidance (Proverbs 3:5-6)

Verse:

"Trust in the Lord with all your heart and lean not on your own understanding; in all your ways submit to him, and he will make your paths straight."

Life is filled with crossroads, moments where we are forced to make decisions without knowing the full picture. These moments can create immense stress, as we grapple with uncertainty and fear of making the wrong choice. Proverbs 3:5-6 offers a remedy for this inner turmoil: trust in the Lord wholeheartedly. This verse invites us to move beyond our limited perspective and rely on God's infinite wisdom.

Trusting God is an act of surrender. It means choosing to let go of our need for control and believing that He is guiding us, even when we can't see the entire path. The instruction to "lean not on your own understanding" is a gentle reminder that our perspective is finite and often clouded by emotions or limited knowledge. God, in contrast, sees the end from the beginning. When we submit to Him, we are aligning ourselves with His perfect plan.

The Challenge of Trusting Fully

Trusting God is easier said than done. It requires us to confront the pride and fear that often drive us to rely on our own understanding. Pride tells us we can handle things on our own, while fear whispers that God may not come through. Proverbs 3:5-6 challenges these lies by calling us to trust with "all our heart." This is not partial trust or trust with conditions—it is a complete surrender of our plans, timelines, and expectations.

This verse also emphasizes submission in "all your ways." Submission involves more than just asking God for guidance; it means being willing to follow where He leads, even when it's uncomfortable or unexpected. The promise is clear: when we trust and submit to God, He will make our paths straight. This doesn't mean life will be free of obstacles, but it assures us that He will provide clarity and direction.

Practical Steps to Trust in God's Guidance

1. **Seek God in Prayer:**
   Before making decisions, bring your concerns to God in prayer. Ask Him for wisdom and clarity, and trust that He will guide you in His timing.
2. **Immerse Yourself in Scripture:**
   God often speaks through His Word. Spend time reading and meditating on passages that align with your situation. Verses like James 1:5 ("If any of you lacks wisdom, you should ask God...") can reinforce your faith in His guidance.
3. **Release the Need for Immediate Answers:**
   Trust involves patience. Resist the urge to rush into decisions for the sake of control. Instead, wait for God's peace to affirm your path.
4. **Reflect on His Faithfulness:**
   Recall times in the past when God guided you through uncertainty. Let these memories strengthen your confidence in His ability to lead you again.

Living Without Leaning on Your Own Understanding

Leaning on our understanding often leads to stress and confusion. We analyze, overthink, and try to predict outcomes, only to feel more overwhelmed. Trusting God means stepping back from this cycle and allowing Him to take the lead. When we lean on Him, we find rest for our minds and peace for our hearts.

Imagine a person navigating a dense forest with no map or compass. Without guidance, they may wander aimlessly, unsure of which path leads to safety. Now picture them receiving a guide who knows the forest intimately. Trusting that guide changes everything—they no longer have to rely on their limited understanding. This is the kind of trust Proverbs 3:5-6 calls us to cultivate with God.

A Testimony of Trust

A man facing a career change felt paralyzed by the fear of the unknown. He had two job offers but didn't know which one to choose. After praying over Proverbs 3:5-6, he surrendered the decision to God, asking for His direction. Within days, one of the companies reached out with a unique opportunity that aligned perfectly with his skills and passions. This experience reminded him that God's guidance often comes in ways we don't expect but always leads to what's best.

Reflection on Proverbs 3:5-6

Think about a decision or challenge you're facing. Are you leaning on your own understanding, or are you seeking God's guidance? Take a moment to pray, inviting Him into the situation. Write down any fears or uncertainties you have, and ask Him to replace them with His wisdom and peace.

Walking in Trust

Trusting God is not a one-time event; it's a daily practice. As you navigate life's twists and turns, let Proverbs 3:5-6 remind you that you don't have to figure everything out on your own. When you trust in the Lord and submit to Him, He will guide your steps, bringing clarity and confidence to your journey. Lean on Him, and watch as He makes your paths straight.

Chapter 9: Overcoming Fear in the Darkest Valleys (Psalm 23:4)

Verse:

"Even though I walk through the darkest valley, I will fear no evil, for you are with me; your rod and your staff, they comfort me."

Life's darkest valleys are often where fear feels most at home. These valleys—marked by loss, uncertainty, or pain—can overwhelm us with feelings of vulnerability and hopelessness. Yet, Psalm 23:4 offers a striking image of courage and comfort. Even in the shadow of death, the psalmist declares, "I will fear no evil." Why? Because God's presence transforms even the darkest valleys into places of reassurance and peace.

This verse doesn't promise that we'll never face hardship. Instead, it acknowledges that valleys are a part of life. What sets believers apart is the knowledge that we never walk through them alone. God's rod and staff, symbols of His guidance and protection, are with us every step of the way. His presence doesn't just lessen our fear—it eradicates it.

God's Presence in the Valley

Fear often thrives in isolation. When we believe we're alone in our struggles, anxiety takes root. Psalm 23:4 dismantles this lie with the assurance that God is always with us. His rod, used by shepherds to protect their sheep, symbolizes His power to defend us from harm. His staff, a tool for guiding and rescuing, represents His ability to lead us safely through the most treacherous terrain.

The promise of God's presence is not just a theoretical concept—it's a deeply personal reality. When we invite Him into our valleys, we experience His peace in ways that surpass understanding. He doesn't always remove the valley, but He equips us to walk through it with confidence.

Fear as a Shadow

The psalmist refers to the "shadow of death," a phrase that captures the fleeting and insubstantial nature of fear. A shadow cannot harm us; it only blocks the light for a moment. When we fix our eyes on God, the source of all light, the shadow loses its power. This doesn't mean the valley isn't real—it is—but its grip on us is broken by the presence of our Shepherd.

Practical Ways to Walk Through the Valley with God

1. **Acknowledge the Fear:**
   Denying or suppressing fear only strengthens its hold. Instead, bring your fear to God in prayer. Be honest about what scares you and ask Him to help you trust His presence.
2. **Meditate on God's Promises:**
   Verses like Psalm 23:4 remind us that God is always with us. Repeat these promises aloud during moments of fear to shift your focus from the valley to the Shepherd.
3. **Lean on God's Community:**
   God often works through people to provide comfort and support. Share your struggles with trusted friends or church members who can pray with you and remind you of His faithfulness.
4. **Take Small Steps Forward:**
   Fear can paralyze us, making it difficult to move. Break the journey into small, manageable steps, asking God for the courage to take each one. Trust that He is guiding your path.

God's Guidance Through His Rod and Staff

The rod and staff are not just tools; they are extensions of the Shepherd's care. The rod protects us from external threats, while the staff draws us back when we wander. Together, they provide security and direction. Trusting in these tools allows us to walk with courage, knowing that God is actively working to keep us safe and on course.

A Testimony of God's Presence

A man battling a life-threatening illness shared how Psalm 23:4 became his anchor. Each morning, he recited the verse, focusing on the words, "I will fear no evil." Despite the uncertainty of his prognosis, he experienced an unshakable peace. He described feeling as though God was walking beside him, guiding him through every doctor's visit and treatment. Though the valley was dark, he knew he was not alone.

Reflection on Psalm 23:4

What valley are you walking through today? Write it down and place this verse beside it. Take a moment to reflect on how God's presence changes your perspective. Pray, "Lord, help me to trust You in this valley. Remind me that I am never alone and that Your rod and staff are always guiding and protecting me."

Moving Through the Valley with Confidence

The darkest valleys may challenge us, but they do not define us. With God as our Shepherd, we can walk through them with courage and peace. Let Psalm 23:4 remind you that no matter how deep or shadowed the valley, the light of God's presence is always with you. Trust in His rod and staff, and move forward, knowing that fear has no place in the company of your Shepherd.

Chapter 10: Unbreakable Love (Romans 8:38-39)

Verse:

"For I am convinced that neither death nor life, neither angels nor demons, neither the present nor the future, nor any powers, neither height nor depth, nor anything else in all creation, will be able to separate us from the love of God that is in Christ Jesus our Lord."

Stress and anxiety often whisper lies that we are alone, unloved, or unworthy. They thrive on a sense of separation, convincing us that our struggles are too much for anyone to handle, even God. But Romans 8:38-39 provides an unshakable truth: nothing can separate us from the love of God. This love is not conditional or fleeting—it is eternal and unbreakable, grounded in the sacrifice of Christ Jesus.

Paul, the author of Romans, speaks with absolute conviction. He lists everything that might try to come between us and God's love—death, life, angels, demons, the present, the future, powers, height, depth, and anything else in creation. His comprehensive list leaves no room for doubt. No matter what we face, we remain firmly in the embrace of God's love.

God's Love as a Foundation of Peace

Knowing we are loved is essential for emotional and mental well-being. Love provides security, belonging, and purpose. When we understand the depth and permanence of God's love, we can face life's challenges with confidence, knowing that we are never alone or abandoned. His love is not based on our performance or circumstances but on His unchanging character.

This truth is particularly powerful in moments of stress and anxiety. When we feel overwhelmed, God's love reminds us that we are held, supported, and cherished. It is a love that doesn't falter in the face of our fears or doubts. Instead, it meets us right where we are and offers a steadying hand.

The Lies of Separation

One of the enemy's greatest tactics is to make us feel isolated from God. Stress can amplify this lie, creating a barrier between us and the truth of His love. But Paul's words in Romans 8 dismantle this deception. They remind us that no circumstance, spiritual force, or personal failing can remove us from God's love. Even when we feel distant, His love is as close as our next breath.

Practical Steps to Embrace God's Love

1. **Meditate on This Truth:**
   Spend time reflecting on Romans 8:38-39. Write the verses down and place them somewhere visible as a daily reminder of God's unbreakable love.
2. **Speak God's Love Over Yourself:**
   In moments of doubt or anxiety, say aloud, "I am loved by God, and nothing can separate me from His love." Hearing these words can reinforce their truth in your heart.
3. **Reflect on Christ's Sacrifice:**
   Jesus' death and resurrection are the ultimate proof of God's love. When you feel unworthy or distant, remind yourself that His love was secured at the cross, and nothing can undo it.
4. **Seek Community:**
   Surround yourself with people who reflect God's love. Their encouragement and support can help reinforce the reality of His presence and care.

Living in the Security of God's Love

When we understand that nothing can separate us from God's love, it changes the way we approach life. Stress and anxiety lose their power because they can no longer isolate us. Instead of being consumed by fear, we can rest in the assurance that we are deeply loved and cared for.

God's love also provides perspective. The challenges we face, while real, are temporary. His love is eternal, and it equips us to endure difficulties with grace and hope. Knowing that we are anchored in His love allows us to face each day with renewed strength.

A Testimony of God's Love in Action

A woman going through a painful divorce shared how Romans 8:38-39 became her lifeline. Feeling unworthy and rejected, she turned to this passage and was reminded of God's constant, unshakable love. As she meditated on these verses, her perspective shifted. Though her circumstances were still painful, she began to see herself as loved and valued by God. This newfound confidence helped her rebuild her life and lean on His love for strength.

Reflection on Romans 8:38-39

What situations or fears make you feel distant from God's love? Write them down and place them beside this verse. Pray, "Lord, remind me of Your unbreakable love. Help me to trust in Your presence, even when I feel overwhelmed."

Walking in God's Love

Nothing in all creation can separate you from God's love. Let this truth anchor you as you navigate stress and anxiety. When life feels heavy, remember that you are deeply loved by the One who holds the universe in His hands. His love is your foundation, your comfort, and your strength. Walk in the assurance that no matter what comes your way, His love is always with you.

Chapter 11: God's Plan for Your Future (Jeremiah 29:11)

Verse:

"For I know the plans I have for you," declares the Lord, "plans to prosper you and not to harm you, plans to give you hope and a future."

When life feels uncertain, stress and anxiety often take the driver's seat. The unknown can make us question our purpose, decisions, and even God's intentions. Jeremiah 29:11, however, offers a resounding promise: God has a plan for us—a plan designed to prosper, not harm; to give us hope and a future. These words remind us that even in the midst of chaos, God is working for our good.

This verse was spoken to the Israelites during a time of exile, a season of suffering and displacement. Though their circumstances were bleak, God's promise pointed to a hopeful future. In the same way, this verse invites us to trust that, no matter how challenging our current situation may be, God is orchestrating something far greater than we can imagine.

God's Perspective vs. Ours

One of the greatest sources of stress is our limited perspective. We see only fragments of the bigger picture, which can lead to frustration and doubt when things don't go as planned. Jeremiah 29:11 reminds us that God's view is infinite. He knows every twist and turn of our lives and is weaving them together for a greater purpose.

The word "prosper" in this verse doesn't necessarily refer to material wealth or success. Instead, it speaks to well-being, spiritual growth, and fulfillment in God's purpose. His plans are not about giving us everything we want but about shaping us into the people He created us to be. Trusting His plan means letting go of our need to control outcomes and believing that He knows what's best for us.

Practical Ways to Trust God's Plan

1. **Focus on the Present:**
   While it's natural to think about the future, dwelling on it can lead to unnecessary worry. Instead, ask yourself, "What is God asking me to do today?" Taking small, faithful steps in the present can lead to big changes over time.
2. **Pray for Guidance:**
   Regularly bring your hopes, fears, and plans to God in prayer. Ask Him to align your desires with His will and to reveal the next steps you should take.
3. **Embrace the Detours:**
   Life rarely goes according to plan, but that doesn't mean God isn't at work. Detours often lead to growth and unexpected blessings. Instead of resisting them, ask God what He wants to teach you during these moments.
4. **Meditate on God's Promises:**
   Write down verses like Jeremiah 29:11 and reflect on them daily. Let them remind you of God's faithfulness and His commitment to your future.

Living with Hope and Purpose

Understanding that God has a plan for your life can transform how you approach stress and anxiety. Instead of feeling trapped by uncertainty, you can lean into the assurance that God is in control. His plans are not random or reactionary—they are intentional and purposeful, designed to lead you into the future He has prepared for you.

When we align ourselves with God's plan, we find peace, even in the waiting. This doesn't mean life will be without challenges, but it does mean we can face those challenges with confidence, knowing that God is working everything together for our good (Romans 8:28).

A Story of Trusting God's Plan

A college graduate struggling to find a job felt defeated after months of rejection. She clung to Jeremiah 29:11, praying for clarity and trusting that God had a plan. One day, she received an unexpected opportunity in a field she had never considered. That job turned out to be a stepping stone to her dream career. Looking back, she realized that God's plan, though different from her own, was far better than she could have imagined.

Reflection on Jeremiah 29:11

What areas of your life feel uncertain or out of control? Write them down and place this verse beside them. Pray, "Lord, help me to trust Your plan for my life. Give me patience and peace as I wait for Your direction."

Walking into Your Future with Confidence

God's plans are always good, even when they don't match our expectations. As you face life's uncertainties, let Jeremiah 29:11 remind you that your future is secure in His hands. Trust in His timing, follow His lead, and rest in the hope that He is preparing something beautiful for you. No matter what challenges you encounter, remember that His plans are to prosper you, to give you hope, and to guide you into a bright future.

Chapter 12: God as Our Refuge and Strength (Psalm 46:1)

Verse:

"God is our refuge and strength, an ever-present help in trouble."

Stress has a way of making us feel exposed and vulnerable. When the pressures of life mount, we search for safety—something or someone to shield us from the storm. Psalm 46:1 offers us that assurance. God is described as both our refuge and our strength, providing shelter and fortitude during life's most challenging moments. His presence is not distant or conditional; it is ever-present, a constant source of help when we need it most.

This verse speaks directly to the human need for security. A refuge is a place of safety, protection, and rest. It's where we go when we feel overwhelmed by the chaos around us. Strength, on the other hand, empowers us to keep going, to stand firm in the face of adversity. Together, these descriptions paint a picture of God as both a sanctuary and a source of resilience.

Finding Refuge in God

Life often feels like a relentless storm, with waves of stress and anxiety threatening to pull us under. When we try to weather the storm on our own, we quickly find ourselves exhausted and defeated. Psalm 46:1 reminds us that we don't have to face life's challenges alone. God invites us to take refuge in Him, to rest in His presence and trust in His protection.

Seeking refuge in God doesn't mean escaping reality or ignoring problems. Instead, it's about finding a safe space in His presence where we can regain perspective and strength. It's in this refuge that we are reminded of who God is—a protector, provider, and ever-present help.

God as Our Strength

While refuge offers shelter, strength equips us to face the storm. God doesn't just protect us from trouble; He empowers us to overcome it. His strength is not something we muster on our own—it's a divine gift, given to those who trust in Him. When we feel weak, God's strength becomes our anchor, enabling us to persevere and find peace even in the midst of turmoil.

Practical Steps to Experience God as Refuge and Strength

1. **Create a Quiet Space for Prayer:**
   When stress overwhelms you, retreat to a quiet place where you can connect with God. Use this time to share your fears and invite Him to be your refuge and strength.
2. **Meditate on God's Promises:**
   Reflect on scriptures like Psalm 46:1, repeating them aloud if necessary. Let these words remind you of God's constant presence and power.
3. **Rely on God in Daily Challenges:**
   In moments of difficulty, pause and ask, "God, how can I lean on You right now?" Trust that He is ready to provide the strength you need.
4. **Practice Gratitude in the Storm:**
   Acknowledge God's presence and provision, even in challenging times. Gratitude shifts your focus from the storm to the One who is carrying you through it.

The Ever-Present Help of God

One of the most comforting aspects of this verse is the promise of God's presence. He is not a distant deity who observes our struggles from afar. He is an ever-present help, actively involved in our lives. This means that no matter where we are or what we're facing, God is with us, ready to guide, protect, and strengthen.

A Story of Refuge and Strength

A single father juggling work, parenting, and financial stress found himself on the verge of collapse. One night, he read Psalm 46:1 and decided to pray for God's help. He began setting aside time each morning to ask for strength and guidance. Over time, he noticed a change—not in his circumstances, but in his ability to face them. He found renewed energy and peace, knowing that God was his refuge and strength.

Reflection on Psalm 46:1

What challenges are you facing today? Take a moment to write them down and reflect on how God can be your refuge and strength in each situation. Pray, "Lord, I come to You for shelter and strength. Help me to trust in Your ever-present help and to find peace in Your presence."

Walking in God's Refuge and Strength

Life's storms are inevitable, but they don't have to overwhelm us. With God as our refuge and strength, we can face any challenge with confidence and peace. Let Psalm 46:1 remind you that you are never alone. No matter how fierce the storm, you have a safe place to run to and the strength to endure. Trust in His presence, and let Him be your anchor in every season of life.

Chapter 13: Courage Through the Spirit (2 Timothy 1:7)

Verse:

"For the Spirit God gave us does not make us timid, but gives us power, love, and self-discipline."

Fear is a powerful force. It can silence dreams, stifle growth, and convince us to shrink away from the opportunities and challenges God places before us. But 2 Timothy 1:7 delivers a liberating truth: fear is not from God. Instead, He equips us with a Spirit of power, love, and self-discipline, enabling us to live boldly and confidently in His purpose.

Paul wrote these words to Timothy, a young leader in the early church, encouraging him to step into his calling with courage. Timothy likely faced opposition and uncertainty, much like we do when confronted with stress and anxiety. This verse is a reminder that the Holy Spirit within us is greater than the fears we face. It calls us to replace timidity with the boldness that comes from God's Spirit.

The Nature of God's Spirit

The Spirit God gives is not timid or hesitant—it is powerful. This power isn't about physical strength or dominance; it's a divine empowerment to face life's challenges with confidence and faith. It's the assurance that God is working in and through us, even when circumstances seem overwhelming.

Love, another attribute of God's Spirit, enables us to act selflessly and compassionately, even in difficult situations. When stress and fear threaten to isolate us, love draws us toward connection and understanding. Self-discipline, the final attribute mentioned, is the ability to remain focused and steady, resisting the pull of anxiety and chaos.

These three attributes—power, love, and self-discipline—work together to equip us for life's challenges. They allow us to respond to stress not with panic, but with purpose and peace.

Overcoming Timidity

Timidity often stems from self-doubt, the belief that we are not enough or that failure is inevitable. But God's Spirit counters this narrative by reminding us of who we are in Christ. We are children of God, equipped and empowered to fulfill His plans. This truth transforms fear into faith, allowing us to step forward with courage.

When we lean into the Spirit of power, love, and self-discipline, we begin to see fear for what it truly is: a distraction. Fear loses its grip when we shift our focus from our limitations to God's limitless strength.

Practical Steps to Live in Power, Love, and Self-Discipline

1. **Pray for Boldness:**
   Ask God to fill you with His Spirit of power, love, and self-discipline. In moments of fear, pause and pray, inviting the Holy Spirit to guide your thoughts and actions.
2. **Practice Self-Discipline Daily:**
   Build habits that reinforce your faith, such as regular prayer, scripture reading, and acts of kindness. These disciplines help you remain grounded and focused, even in stressful situations.
3. **Act in Love:**

When fear tempts you to withdraw or react harshly, choose love instead. Look for ways to serve and encourage others, shifting your perspective from inward anxiety to outward compassion.

4. **Recall God's Faithfulness:**
   Reflect on times when God gave you the strength to overcome challenges. Let these memories remind you of His power and presence in your life.

The Role of Faith in Fearlessness

Faith doesn't eliminate fear, but it gives us the courage to face it. By trusting in the Spirit God has given us, we can approach life with boldness and clarity. The power, love, and self-discipline within us are not of our own making—they are gifts from God, given to equip us for every trial and triumph.

A Story of Boldness Through the Spirit

A young teacher struggling with public speaking feared she wouldn't connect with her students. She began praying 2 Timothy 1:7 daily, asking God for boldness. Over time, she noticed a shift in her confidence. Instead of focusing on her fears, she leaned into the Spirit of power and love. Her newfound courage not only improved her teaching but also inspired her students to face their own challenges with confidence.

Reflection on 2 Timothy 1:7

What areas of your life are held back by fear? Write them down and place this verse beside them. Pray, "Lord, help me to live in the Spirit You have given me. Replace my timidity with Your power, love, and self-discipline."

Living Fearlessly in God's Spirit

God has not given us a spirit of fear. Instead, He has equipped us with everything we need to face life's challenges with courage and grace. Let 2 Timothy 1:7 remind you that you are not defined by timidity or hesitation. You are empowered by the Spirit of God to live boldly, love deeply, and remain steady in every situation. Step into your calling with confidence, knowing that His Spirit is with you.

Chapter 14: Rest for the Weary (Matthew 11:28-30)

Verse:

"Come to me, all you who are weary and burdened, and I will give you rest. Take my yoke upon you and learn from me, for I am gentle and humble in heart, and you will find rest for your souls. For my yoke is easy and my burden is light."

Weariness is a feeling that goes beyond physical exhaustion. It's the weight of carrying too many burdens—mental, emotional, and spiritual—that leaves us depleted and overwhelmed. In Matthew 11:28-30, Jesus extends a powerful invitation to those who feel crushed by life's demands. He offers rest, not just for the body but for the soul, promising to share the load we carry and replace it with His gentle, life-giving presence.

These verses remind us that we don't have to navigate stress and anxiety alone. Jesus doesn't demand that we fix ourselves before coming to Him. Instead, He calls us to come as we are—broken, weary, and burdened—and promises to provide the rest and renewal we desperately need.

The Yoke of Christ

Jesus uses the metaphor of a yoke, a farming tool that binds two animals together to share the load of pulling a plow. On its own, a single animal would struggle to pull the weight, but with a yoke, the burden becomes manageable. When Jesus says, "Take my yoke upon you," He is inviting us into a partnership where He bears the brunt of the load, guiding and supporting us every step of the way.

His yoke is not like the burdens we often place on ourselves—self-imposed expectations, perfectionism, or the need to control every detail of our lives. Instead, His yoke is easy, and His burden is light because it is carried in love and grace. In walking alongside Him, we learn not only how to rest but also how to live with greater peace and purpose.

The Rest Jesus Offers

The rest Jesus promises goes beyond physical relief. It is a deep, soul-level rest that brings renewal and clarity. This rest doesn't mean an absence of challenges but rather a reprieve from the constant striving and stress that so often define our lives. When we accept His invitation, we find a peace that transcends circumstances and a strength that sustains us through life's trials.

Practical Ways to Find Rest in Jesus

1. **Come to Him in Prayer:**
   Begin each day by bringing your burdens to Jesus. Be honest about what's weighing you down and ask Him to help you carry the load.
2. **Practice Sabbath Rest:**
   Set aside one day a week to rest and focus on God. Use this time to recharge physically, emotionally, and spiritually by stepping away from work and reconnecting with Him.
3. **Let Go of Perfectionism:**
   Reflect on areas where you're striving for unattainable standards. Surrender these to Jesus and ask Him to guide you in embracing grace over perfection.
4. **Meditate on His Promises:**
   Reflect on verses like Matthew 11:28-30, allowing His words to remind you that rest is not only a gift but also a necessity for your well-being.

Learning from Jesus

Jesus describes Himself as gentle and humble in heart. These qualities make Him a compassionate teacher who understands our struggles. As we walk with Him, we learn how to approach life with a calm and steady spirit, trusting in His guidance rather than our own efforts. His humility reminds us that we don't have to be perfect to receive His love, and His gentleness invites us to rest in His presence without fear of judgment.

A Testimony of Restored Peace

A mother juggling a demanding job and family responsibilities found herself on the brink of burnout. One morning, she read Matthew 11:28-30 and decided to pray, asking Jesus to help her carry her burdens. She began incorporating moments of rest into her week—prayer walks, quiet time with scripture, and letting go of unnecessary tasks. Over time, she noticed a profound shift in her perspective. Though her responsibilities hadn't changed, her soul felt lighter, and she found renewed strength to face each day.

Reflection on Matthew 11:28-30

What burdens are you carrying today? Write them down and place them beside this verse. Pray, "Lord, I come to You with my weariness and burdens. Teach me to take Your yoke and find rest for my soul. Help me to trust in Your guidance and grace."

Walking in His Rest

Jesus' invitation to rest is not a one-time offer—it is a daily practice. As you navigate the demands of life, let Matthew 11:28-30 remind you that you don't have to carry everything on your own. Take His yoke, learn from Him, and find the rest your soul longs for. In His gentle and humble presence, you will discover a peace that sustains you through every challenge.

Chapter 15: Perfect Peace Through Trust (Isaiah 26:3)

Verse:

"You will keep in perfect peace those whose minds are steadfast, because they trust in you."

Peace is something many people long for but few seem to find. In a world filled with endless distractions, responsibilities, and uncertainties, peace often feels like an elusive dream. Yet Isaiah 26:3 presents a powerful promise: perfect peace is available to those who keep their minds focused on God and trust in Him completely.

This verse describes not just any peace but *perfect peace*—a state of wholeness and completeness that transcends circumstances. It is the kind of peace that steadies your heart in the middle of a storm, that allows you to rest even when life feels chaotic. This peace doesn't come from external sources or temporary solutions. It is a gift from God, sustained by trusting in His unchanging character and faithfulness.

What Does It Mean to Be Steadfast?

The word "steadfast" implies focus and determination. It means keeping your thoughts fixed on God, even when everything around you tries to pull your attention elsewhere. This kind of focus requires intentionality. It's about choosing to dwell on His promises rather than your problems, to meditate on His faithfulness instead of your fears.

Being steadfast doesn't mean denying reality or pretending everything is fine. Instead, it means acknowledging your challenges while anchoring your mind in the truth of who God is. Trusting Him becomes the foundation for peace, even when life feels uncertain.

The Connection Between Trust and Peace

Trust is at the heart of this promise. When we trust God, we release the need to control every detail of our lives. We let go of the "what-ifs" and "what-now" questions that fuel anxiety. Trusting God doesn't mean we have all the answers; it means we believe that He does.

When our minds are fixed on God, fear and worry lose their grip. Instead of being consumed by stress, we find ourselves grounded in the assurance that God is in control. This trust doesn't eliminate challenges, but it changes how we face them. With God at the center of our thoughts, peace becomes a natural response.

Practical Steps to Cultivate Perfect Peace

1. **Start Each Day with God:**
   Begin your morning by focusing your mind on God. Read a scripture, pray, or meditate on a promise like Isaiah 26:3. Let His truth set the tone for your day.
2. **Redirect Negative Thoughts:**
   When worry or fear arises, pause and consciously shift your focus to God. Remind yourself of His faithfulness and repeat a verse like, "You will keep in perfect peace those whose minds are steadfast."
3. **Practice Gratitude:**
   Gratitude helps align your mind with God's goodness. Make a habit of listing things you're thankful for each day, even in challenging circumstances.
4. **Limit Distractions:**
   Reduce the noise in your life that competes for your attention. This might mean setting boundaries with social

media, news, or other stress-inducing activities, and replacing them with time spent in prayer or worship.

Perfect Peace in Action

Perfect peace doesn't mean life is free of trouble. It means that in the middle of those troubles, you have a steady confidence in God's care. This peace allows you to make decisions with clarity, build relationships without fear, and approach challenges with resilience.

Consider the imagery of a bird resting on a branch during a storm. The bird's peace doesn't come from the storm ending; it comes from knowing the branch is strong enough to hold it. In the same way, our peace comes from trusting that God is strong enough to sustain us, no matter what we face.

A Testimony of Perfect Peace

A man navigating a difficult season of unemployment struggled with anxiety about his future. Each morning, he began reading Isaiah 26:3 and meditating on God's faithfulness. Over time, he noticed a shift in his mindset. While the uncertainty of his circumstances remained, his heart felt steady and at peace. He later described this period as one of the most spiritually fulfilling times of his life, as it deepened his trust in God.

Reflection on Isaiah 26:3

What thoughts tend to dominate your mind during stressful times? Take a moment to write them down and pray over them. Ask God to help you shift your focus to Him. Pray, "Lord, keep my mind steadfast on You. Help me to trust You fully so I can experience Your perfect peace."

Walking in Perfect Peace

Perfect peace is not reserved for a select few—it is available to all who fix their minds on God and trust in Him. As you navigate the ups and downs of life, let Isaiah 26:3 remind you that peace is possible, no matter your circumstances. Keep your thoughts centered on Him, and allow His unchanging presence to fill your heart with calm and confidence.

Chapter 16: Casting Out Fear with Love (1 John 4:18)

Verse:

"There is no fear in love. But perfect love drives out fear, because fear has to do with punishment. The one who fears is not made perfect in love."

Fear often feels like an inevitable part of life, whispering doubts, insecurities, and uncertainties into our minds. It keeps us stuck, preventing us from fully embracing opportunities, relationships, and even our faith. But 1 John 4:18 offers a profound truth: fear and love cannot coexist. God's perfect love is so powerful that it drives out fear, replacing it with security, peace, and freedom.

This verse points us to the heart of God's relationship with us. His love is not conditional or based on performance. It is complete, unchanging, and perfect. When we fully grasp this love, fear loses its hold. Fear thrives on punishment and the anticipation of negative outcomes. Love, however, assures us of God's goodness, His forgiveness, and His commitment to our well-being. To live in perfect love is to live free from fear.

The Nature of Perfect Love

Perfect love is not something we achieve through effort; it is a gift from God. This love is rooted in His character and demonstrated through Jesus' sacrifice on the cross. It is a love that says, "You are mine, and nothing can separate you from Me." When we embrace this truth, we begin to see fear for what it truly is—a liar that has no place in the life of someone loved by God.

Fear often masquerades as caution or self-protection, but at its core, it is a barrier to trust. It convinces us that we are on our own, that we have to control everything, or that failure is inevitable. Perfect love dismantles these lies. It reminds us that we are not alone, that God is in control, and that His plans for us are good.

Replacing Fear with Love

Living in the freedom of God's love requires intentionality. It means choosing to focus on His promises instead of our fears. It means inviting His love into the areas of our lives where fear has taken root and allowing Him to transform our perspective.

Practical Steps to Cast Out Fear with Love

1. **Immerse Yourself in God's Love:**
   Spend time reading scriptures about God's love, such as Romans 8:38-39 or John 3:16. Let these verses remind you of His unwavering commitment to you.
2. **Speak Truth to Fear:**
   When fear arises, counter it with God's promises. Say aloud, "Perfect love drives out fear," and affirm that God's love is greater than any worry or doubt.
3. **Reflect on Christ's Sacrifice:**
   The cross is the ultimate demonstration of God's love. When you feel unworthy or afraid, remember that Jesus' sacrifice was for you. His love is the foundation of your freedom.
4. **Pray for a Heart of Love:**
   Ask God to fill you with His love, not only for yourself but also for others. Fear diminishes when we focus on loving and serving those around us.

Living in Freedom from Fear

God's perfect love transforms how we see ourselves, our circumstances, and our future. When we fully embrace His love, we stop striving to earn approval or avoid failure. Instead, we live with confidence, knowing that we are held securely in His hands. Fear may still try to creep in, but it can no longer dictate our decisions or steal our peace.

Love also compels us to act boldly. When fear is removed, we can step into our purpose with courage. Whether it's pursuing a new opportunity, sharing our faith, or deepening relationships, God's love empowers us to move forward without hesitation.

A Testimony of Fear Overcome by Love

A young man battling anxiety about starting a new business was paralyzed by the fear of failure. He began studying 1 John 4:18, praying for God to replace his fear with a deep understanding of His love. Over time, the assurance of God's love gave him the courage to take the first steps toward his dream. Though challenges arose, he approached each one with confidence, knowing that God's love was greater than his fears.

Reflection on 1 John 4:18

What fears are holding you back today? Write them down and pray over them, asking God to fill those spaces with His perfect love. Pray, "Lord, help me to live in the freedom of Your love. Cast out the fears that try to control me and replace them with the peace and security of Your presence."

Walking in the Confidence of God's Love

Fear has no place in a heart that is filled with God's perfect love. As you navigate life's uncertainties, let 1 John 4:18 remind you that God's love is greater than any fear. Step forward in confidence, knowing that His love is unchanging, His plans are good, and His presence is with you always. Live boldly, free from fear, and fully embraced by His perfect love.

Chapter 17: Strength in Weakness (2 Corinthians 12:9)

Verse:

"But he said to me, 'My grace is sufficient for you, for my power is made perfect in weakness.' Therefore I will boast all the more gladly about my weaknesses, so that Christ's power may rest on me."

Weakness is often something we try to hide. Society celebrates strength, competence, and independence, leaving little room for vulnerability. Yet, 2 Corinthians 12:9 presents a radically different perspective: it is in our weakness that God's power is most evident. Paul's words invite us to stop striving for perfection and instead rest in the sufficiency of God's grace.

This verse was written in the context of Paul's struggles—his "thorn in the flesh," as he described it. Despite pleading with God to remove this hardship, Paul received an unexpected answer: the grace of God was enough. Rather than eliminating the weakness, God chose to work through it, demonstrating that His power is not diminished by human frailty. Instead, it shines all the brighter against the backdrop of our limitations.

God's Power in Our Weakness

Weakness is not a flaw to be fixed but an opportunity for God's strength to be revealed. When we acknowledge our limitations, we make space for His power to work in and through us. This doesn't mean we resign ourselves to defeat; it means we shift our focus from what we can't do to what God can do.

Grace is the key to this transformation. God's grace is not only sufficient—it is abundant, overflowing, and tailored to meet our every need. It equips us to face challenges with confidence, knowing that we are not relying on our own strength but on His.

Embracing Weakness as a Path to Strength

Admitting weakness can feel counterintuitive, especially in a world that prizes self-reliance. But when we let go of the pressure to have it all together, we discover a freedom that comes from trusting God completely. Our weaknesses are not obstacles to His plans; they are tools He uses to display His glory.

Practical Steps to Embrace God's Strength in Weakness

1. **Acknowledge Your Limitations:**
   Take an honest inventory of the areas where you feel weak or inadequate. Instead of seeing these as failures, view them as opportunities for God to show His power.
2. **Pray for God's Strength:**
   In moments of struggle, ask God to fill you with His grace and strength. Be specific about your needs, trusting that His power is more than sufficient.
3. **Celebrate Progress, Not Perfection:**
   Focus on the ways God is working in your life, even if progress feels small. Remember that His power is most evident in the process, not just the outcome.
4. **Share Your Testimony:**
   Open up about your struggles with others. Sharing how God has worked through your weaknesses can inspire and encourage those around you.

Grace in Action

God's grace is not just a theological concept—it is a practical, sustaining force. It meets us in our everyday struggles, giving us the strength to persevere. When we rely on His grace, we find that even our weakest moments can be transformed into powerful testimonies of His love and faithfulness.

Consider the image of a cracked clay jar. Though it may seem flawed, the cracks allow light to shine through, illuminating everything around it. In the same way, our weaknesses allow God's light to shine more brightly, drawing others to His goodness.

A Story of Strength in Weakness

A woman battling chronic illness often felt defeated by her physical limitations. She began meditating on 2 Corinthians 12:9, praying for God's strength to carry her through each day. Over time, she found a new sense of purpose. Though her illness remained, she started sharing her story with others, encouraging them to trust in God's grace. Her weakness became a platform for His power, touching lives in ways she never imagined.

Reflection on 2 Corinthians 12:9

What weaknesses are you struggling with today? Write them down and place this verse beside them. Pray, "Lord, I surrender my weaknesses to You. Let Your grace sustain me and Your power work through me. Help me to trust in Your sufficiency."

Walking in God's Power

Weakness is not the end of the story—it is the beginning of God's work in your life. Let 2 Corinthians 12:9 remind you that His grace is sufficient for every challenge you face. Embrace your limitations as opportunities for His power to shine, and trust that His strength will carry you through. In your weakness, you will find His grace, His peace, and His perfect strength.

Chapter 18: Strength Through Patience (Isaiah 40:31)

Verse:

"But those who hope in the Lord will renew their strength. They will soar on wings like eagles; they will run and not grow weary, they will walk and not be faint."

Patience can feel like one of the hardest virtues to practice, especially in the face of stress and anxiety. Life often demands immediate answers, results, and resolutions, leaving us frustrated when things don't happen on our timeline. Yet, Isaiah 40:31 reminds us that waiting on the Lord is not passive—it is a transformative act of faith that renews our strength and empowers us to rise above life's challenges.

This verse offers three vivid images of renewal: soaring like eagles, running without weariness, and walking without fainting. Each represents a unique aspect of God's provision. Sometimes, He gives us the strength to soar above our circumstances. Other times, He equips us to run through them with endurance. And in quieter moments, He helps us take steady steps forward. No matter the season, God's strength meets us exactly where we are.

What It Means to Hope in the Lord

Hoping in the Lord is not simply wishing for a better outcome. It is an active trust in His timing, promises, and character. This hope requires us to relinquish control and place our confidence in God's ability to work all things for our good. It's a declaration that, even when we don't see the full picture, we trust the One who holds it.

Waiting on the Lord also involves aligning our expectations with His will. It's about seeking His direction and allowing His strength to sustain us, rather than relying on our own limited resources.

The Renewal of Strength

Renewal is the process of being restored, refreshed, and re-energized. When we wait on God, we allow Him to replenish what stress and worry have depleted. This renewal is not just physical—it's emotional, mental, and spiritual. It enables us to face life's demands with resilience and peace.

The image of an eagle soaring is particularly powerful. Eagles don't flap their wings tirelessly; they glide on air currents, letting the wind carry them higher. In the same way, God invites us to rest in His strength, allowing Him to lift us above the weight of our struggles.

Practical Ways to Wait on the Lord

1. **Cultivate Stillness:**
   Create space in your day to be still before God. Use this time to pray, meditate on scripture, or simply listen for His voice. Stillness allows you to release stress and receive His peace.
2. **Focus on God's Promises:**
   Reflect on verses like Isaiah 40:31 and remind yourself of God's faithfulness. Let His promises anchor your hope and renew your strength.
3. **Practice Patience in Small Things:**
   Use everyday moments—like waiting in line or sitting in traffic—as opportunities to practice patience. These small acts of trust can build your capacity to wait on God in larger areas of life.
4. **Seek Strength in Community:**
   Surround yourself with people who encourage and support

your faith journey. Their prayers and encouragement can help sustain you as you wait on the Lord.

Living with Renewed Strength

Waiting on the Lord is not easy, but it is always worth it. When we trust in Him, we find a strength that surpasses human understanding. This strength enables us to rise above our circumstances, persevere through challenges, and move forward with confidence. It shifts our perspective from what we lack to what God provides.

Consider the metaphor of running a marathon. Without proper training and nourishment, a runner quickly grows weary. But with preparation and support, they can endure to the finish line. In the same way, waiting on the Lord renews our spiritual endurance, equipping us to run life's race with unwavering faith.

A Testimony of Strength Renewed

A man recovering from a long period of unemployment felt drained by the constant rejection and uncertainty. He began meditating on Isaiah 40:31, asking God to renew his strength. As he waited on the Lord, he found new opportunities to volunteer and connect with others, which reignited his sense of purpose. Eventually, he secured a job that aligned with his skills and passions. Looking back, he realized that the waiting period had strengthened his faith and prepared him for the next chapter.

Reflection on Isaiah 40:31

What areas of your life require patience and renewed strength? Write them down and place this verse beside them. Pray, "Lord, teach me to wait on You. Renew my strength and help me trust in Your timing. Lift me up with Your power so I can soar above my circumstances."

Soaring with God's Strength

Life's demands can leave us weary, but God promises renewal to those who place their hope in Him. Let Isaiah 40:31 remind you that waiting on the Lord is not a passive act—it is a powerful expression of trust. As you wait, He will renew your strength, helping you to soar, run, and walk without fainting. Trust in His timing, and allow His presence to carry you through every season.

Chapter 19: A Refuge in Times of Trouble (Nahum 1:7)

Verse:

"The Lord is good, a refuge in times of trouble. He cares for those who trust in Him."

Life is unpredictable, and trouble often comes when we least expect it. These moments can leave us feeling vulnerable, unsure of where to turn. Nahum 1:7 offers a powerful reminder of God's unchanging goodness and His role as our refuge. When the storms of life rage, He is our safe haven, providing shelter, care, and strength.

This verse highlights three essential truths: God's goodness, His availability as a refuge, and His care for those who trust in Him. Together, they form a foundation of hope and assurance for anyone navigating difficult seasons.

The Goodness of God

At the core of this verse is the declaration of God's goodness. His goodness is not dependent on circumstances—it is an unchanging aspect of His character. Even when life feels chaotic or unfair, God remains good. This truth gives us a solid foundation to stand on when everything else seems uncertain.

Trusting in God's goodness doesn't mean we ignore our pain or pretend that challenges don't exist. Instead, it means we acknowledge that, even in the hardest moments, God is working for our good. His goodness is a source of comfort, reminding us that we are never forgotten or abandoned.

God as Our Refuge

A refuge is a place of safety, protection, and rest. In ancient times, cities of refuge were established to provide shelter for those in danger. Today, God serves as our spiritual refuge, offering peace and security in the face of life's troubles. When we turn to Him, we find a shelter that no storm can destroy.

The idea of God as a refuge emphasizes His closeness. He is not a distant deity observing our struggles from afar. He is present, accessible, and ready to provide the protection and strength we need. Turning to God as our refuge means choosing to rest in His care rather than relying on our own strength.

His Care for Those Who Trust Him

The final part of this verse assures us of God's active care. He doesn't just offer a refuge—He deeply cares for those who place their trust in Him. This care is personal and attentive. God knows our fears, burdens, and needs, and He is committed to walking with us through them.

Trusting in God's care requires surrender. It means releasing our worries and allowing Him to guide and support us. When we place our trust in Him, we experience the peace and comfort that comes from knowing we are held by a loving and powerful God.

Practical Steps to Find Refuge in God

1. **Seek Him in Prayer:**
   When trouble arises, turn to God immediately in prayer. Share your fears and frustrations with Him, trusting that He hears and cares.
2. **Meditate on His Goodness:**
   Reflect on times when you've experienced God's goodness in the past. Let these memories remind you of His faithfulness

and inspire confidence in His care.

3. **Rest in His Presence:**
   Create moments of stillness in your day to rest in God's presence. Whether through worship, scripture reading, or quiet reflection, these moments allow you to experience His refuge.
4. **Trust His Timing:**
   God's care often unfolds in ways we don't expect. Be patient and trust that His plans are good, even when the path is unclear.

Living in God's Refuge

Turning to God as our refuge doesn't eliminate life's challenges, but it changes how we face them. Instead of feeling overwhelmed, we can approach difficulties with confidence, knowing that we are protected and cared for. His goodness becomes a source of strength, and His refuge offers peace in the midst of the storm.

A Testimony of Finding Refuge

A woman facing the sudden loss of her home due to a natural disaster described how Nahum 1:7 became her anchor. In the midst of uncertainty, she turned to God daily, praying for His guidance and protection. Though rebuilding her life was challenging, she found peace in His presence and experienced His care through the support of her community. Looking back, she credited God's refuge as the reason she was able to move forward with hope.

Reflection on Nahum 1:7

What troubles are you facing today? Write them down and place this verse beside them. Pray, "Lord, I trust in Your goodness. Be my refuge in this time of trouble, and remind me of Your care. Help me to rest in Your presence and find peace in Your love."

Walking in His Care

Life's troubles may shake us, but they cannot destroy us when God is our refuge. Let Nahum 1:7 remind you that His goodness is unchanging, His protection is steadfast, and His care is personal. Trust in Him, and rest in the knowledge that He is with you through every storm.

Chapter 20: God's Peace in Every Circumstance (Philippians 4:6-7)

Verse:

"Do not be anxious about anything, but in every situation, by prayer and petition, with thanksgiving, present your requests to God. And the peace of God, which transcends all understanding, will guard your hearts and your minds in Christ Jesus."

Anxiety has a way of gripping our hearts and minds, pulling us into cycles of worry and fear. In Philippians 4:6-7, Paul offers a remedy: prayer, thanksgiving, and trust in God. This passage invites us to trade our anxiety for a peace that surpasses human understanding, a peace that comes directly from God and acts as a shield for our hearts and minds.

These verses don't ignore the reality of life's challenges. Instead, they provide a framework for navigating them with faith. Paul doesn't suggest that we suppress or deny our concerns. Rather, he encourages us to bring every worry to God in prayer, trusting that He is both willing and able to help.

The Power of Prayer

Prayer is the foundation of this passage. When we choose to pray instead of worry, we shift our focus from our problems to God's power. This act of surrender invites Him into our circumstances, allowing His peace to replace our anxiety. Through prayer, we acknowledge that we don't have to face life's challenges alone.

Paul emphasizes the importance of presenting our requests "with thanksgiving." Gratitude changes our perspective, reminding us of God's faithfulness and provision in the past. It helps us approach Him with trust and confidence, knowing that He has already demonstrated His care.

The Peace of God

The peace Paul describes is not dependent on circumstances. It is a divine gift that transcends logic and reason, offering calm and assurance even in the midst of chaos. This peace acts as a guard, protecting our hearts and minds from the constant barrage of worry and fear.

God's peace doesn't mean the absence of problems, but it changes how we experience them. It allows us to face difficulties with resilience and hope, knowing that we are held securely in His hands.

Practical Steps to Experience God's Peace

1. **Turn Worries Into Prayers:**
   Each time a worry arises, stop and turn it into a prayer. Be specific about your concerns and invite God to take control of the situation.
2. **Practice Daily Gratitude:**
   Start a gratitude journal and list three things you're thankful for each day. This practice helps shift your focus from what's wrong to what God is doing.
3. **Meditate on God's Promises:**
   Reflect on scriptures like Philippians 4:6-7, allowing them to remind you of God's faithfulness and peace.
4. **Create a Prayer Routine:**
   Set aside regular times each day to pray and present your requests to God. This discipline helps you build a habit of relying on Him rather than your own strength.

Living Without Anxiety

Choosing not to be anxious is a daily decision. It requires us to surrender our fears to God and trust in His provision. Over time, this practice transforms our hearts and minds, allowing us to experience His peace more fully. When anxiety threatens to overwhelm, we can remind ourselves of this promise: God's peace is greater than any problem we face.

A Testimony of God's Peace

A college student preparing for final exams felt overwhelmed by the pressure to succeed. She began reciting Philippians 4:6-7 each morning, praying for God's peace and thanking Him for His guidance. As she focused on trusting God rather than her circumstances, she noticed a significant shift. Her stress diminished, and she approached her exams with clarity and confidence, experiencing God's peace in a way she had never known before.

Reflection on Philippians 4:6-7

What worries are consuming your thoughts today? Write them down and pray over each one, thanking God for His presence and provision. Pray, "Lord, I bring my worries to You. Replace my anxiety with Your peace, and guard my heart and mind in Christ Jesus."

Walking in God's Peace

Anxiety may try to take root in your heart, but Philippians 4:6-7 reminds you that God's peace is always available. Choose to bring your concerns to Him in prayer, trusting that His peace will guard your heart and mind. In every circumstance, let gratitude and faith guide you as you experience the unshakable peace of God.

Chapter 21: Unwavering Trust in Times of Fear (Psalm 56:3-4)

Verse:

"When I am afraid, I put my trust in you. In God, whose word I praise—in God I trust and am not afraid. What can mere mortals do to me?"

Fear is a natural response to uncertainty, danger, or perceived threats. It grips the heart and clouds the mind, making even the strongest individuals feel vulnerable. Yet, in Psalm 56:3-4, David offers a powerful antidote to fear: trust in God. This passage acknowledges the reality of fear but provides a way to rise above it through faith.

David, the author of this psalm, faced countless moments of danger and adversity. From being pursued by King Saul to fighting in battles, his life was filled with reasons to be afraid. But instead of allowing fear to consume him, David repeatedly chose to place his trust in God. His confidence came not from his own strength but from the unwavering faithfulness of the One he praised.

When Fear Arises

The phrase "When I am afraid" is key. It doesn't say "if" but "when," recognizing that fear is an inevitable part of life. The difference lies in how we respond to it. Instead of letting fear dictate his actions, David made a deliberate choice: "I put my trust in you." This simple yet profound act of faith transformed his perspective and gave him the courage to face his challenges.

Trusting God doesn't mean denying fear's existence—it means refusing to let it control us. It's a decision to shift our focus from the size of the problem to the greatness of God.

The Power of God's Word

David's trust was rooted in God's word. He praised it as the foundation of his faith, drawing strength and reassurance from its promises. When fear arises, immersing ourselves in scripture reminds us of God's faithfulness, His protection, and His sovereignty. It shifts our mindset from fear to faith, grounding us in truths that transcend our circumstances.

Practical Steps to Trust God in Fear

1. **Acknowledge Your Fear:**
   Start by admitting your fear to God. Be honest about what's troubling you and invite Him into the situation.
2. **Declare God's Promises:**
   Speak scriptures like Psalm 56:3-4 aloud. Let the truth of His word replace the lies of fear.
3. **Reflect on Past Deliverance:**
   Recall times when God has helped you overcome challenges. Let these memories remind you of His faithfulness and encourage you to trust Him again.
4. **Take Small Steps of Faith:**
   Fear often paralyzes, making it hard to move forward. Trust God by taking one small step toward the challenge, believing that He will guide and sustain you.

Fearlessness Through Trust

David's rhetorical question, "What can mere mortals do to me?" reflects a deep understanding of God's sovereignty. When we trust in

God, we recognize that no human threat can overpower His plan for our lives. This doesn't mean life will be free of hardships, but it assures us that God's protection and presence are greater than any fear we face.

Living without fear doesn't mean we'll never feel afraid. It means that when fear comes, we respond with trust, allowing God's presence to calm our hearts and guide our steps.

A Testimony of Overcoming Fear

A young man preparing to give his first public speech was consumed with anxiety. He couldn't stop imagining worst-case scenarios. The night before, he read Psalm 56:3-4 and decided to pray every time fear crept in. As he stepped onto the stage, he repeated, "When I am afraid, I put my trust in you." Though nervous, he felt a peace that carried him through the speech. Reflecting on the experience, he realized that trusting God had shifted his focus from fear to faith.

Reflection on Psalm 56:3-4

What fears are you facing today? Write them down and place this verse beside them. Pray, "Lord, I put my trust in You. Help me to face my fears with faith and confidence, knowing that You are with me."

Walking in Trust, Not Fear

Fear may come, but it doesn't have to stay. Psalm 56:3-4 reminds us that trust in God is the path to courage and peace. When fear arises, choose to focus on His promises, His protection, and His faithfulness. In every moment of uncertainty, let this verse guide you as you place your trust in the One who is greater than any fear.

Chapter 22: Victory Through Faith (1 John 5:4)

Verse:

"For everyone born of God overcomes the world. This is the victory that has overcome the world, even our faith."

Life is full of challenges, struggles, and obstacles that often seem insurmountable. Yet 1 John 5:4 reminds us that as children of God, we are not defeated by the world—we overcome it. This victory is not achieved through our own strength or efforts but through our faith in Christ. It is faith that empowers us to rise above adversity, to face difficulties with courage, and to walk in the assurance of God's ultimate triumph.

Faith is not merely believing in God's existence; it is trusting in His power, promises, and plan. It is the lens through which we see our circumstances and the foundation on which we stand when life feels uncertain. This faith is not passive—it is active, persistent, and transformative, equipping us to overcome the challenges of the world.

Born to Overcome

The phrase "everyone born of God" is key to understanding this verse. When we accept Christ, we are spiritually reborn, becoming part of God's family. This new identity comes with the promise of victory—not because of who we are, but because of who He is. As His children, we share in His strength, His authority, and His victory over sin and the world.

Overcoming the world doesn't mean we won't face struggles. Jesus Himself said, "In this world, you will have trouble" (John 16:33). But He also promised, "Take heart! I have overcome the world." Our faith connects us to this victory, enabling us to face challenges with confidence and hope.

Faith as the Source of Victory

Faith is the victory that overcomes the world. It is not a tool to avoid difficulties but a weapon to triumph over them. Faith empowers us to see beyond our circumstances and trust in God's plan, even when we don't understand it. It reminds us that no problem, no fear, and no failure is greater than God's power.

Faith also transforms how we respond to challenges. Instead of being overwhelmed, we face them with resilience, knowing that God is in control. This doesn't mean the journey will be easy, but it assures us that the outcome is secure.

Practical Steps to Live in Victory

1. **Strengthen Your Faith:**
   Spend time in God's Word, prayer, and worship to deepen your relationship with Him. The more you know Him, the stronger your faith will become.
2. **Declare God's Promises:**
   Speak scriptures like 1 John 5:4 aloud during moments of doubt or difficulty. Remind yourself of the victory that is already yours in Christ.
3. **Take Faith-Filled Action:**
   Faith is not passive. Trust God by stepping out in obedience, even when the path ahead seems uncertain. Each act of faith strengthens your connection to His victory.
4. **Celebrate Small Wins:**

> Recognize and thank God for the victories—big and small—that He brings into your life. Gratitude reinforces your faith and helps you see His hand at work.

Living as Overcomers

Living as an overcomer means walking in the truth that your victory is already secure in Christ. It means refusing to let fear, doubt, or failure define you. Instead, you stand firm in your faith, trusting that God is working all things for your good.

Overcoming doesn't mean avoiding challenges—it means facing them with the assurance that God's power is greater than anything the world can throw at you. It's about living with confidence, courage, and hope, knowing that your faith connects you to God's limitless strength.

A Testimony of Victory Through Faith

A man battling addiction felt trapped in a cycle of defeat. He began meditating on 1 John 5:4 and praying for the faith to overcome. Each day, he declared his identity as a child of God and leaned on God's strength to resist temptation. Over time, he experienced freedom, not because the journey was easy, but because his faith gave him the power to persevere. His story became a testimony of God's victory, inspiring others to trust in Him.

Reflection on 1 John 5:4

What challenges are you facing today? Write them down and place this verse beside them. Pray, "Lord, I trust in Your victory. Strengthen my faith and help me to overcome the challenges of this world, knowing that my identity in You makes me an overcomer."

Walking in Victory

Victory is not something you achieve on your own—it is a gift from God, accessed through faith. Let 1 John 5:4 remind you that as His child, you are already victorious. In every trial and triumph, live with the assurance that your faith connects you to the One who has overcome the world. Step forward in confidence, knowing that no challenge is too great for the God who lives within you.

Chapter 23: Courage in the Face of Trials (Joshua 1:9)

Verse:

"Have I not commanded you? Be strong and courageous. Do not be afraid; do not be discouraged, for the Lord your God will be with you wherever you go."

Fear and discouragement are common reactions to life's challenges, especially when the path ahead feels uncertain or overwhelming. In Joshua 1:9, God delivers a clear and empowering command: be strong and courageous. This instruction is not a suggestion or a request—it is a divine mandate rooted in the assurance of His presence. For Joshua, stepping into leadership after Moses' death must have been daunting, yet God's promise of unwavering support gave him the courage to move forward.

This verse applies to anyone facing trials, transitions, or fears. It reminds us that courage is not the absence of fear but the decision to trust God in the midst of it. When we anchor ourselves in His promises, we gain the strength to face life's challenges with confidence and resilience.

God's Command: Be Strong and Courageous

The repeated call to "be strong and courageous" throughout Joshua 1 emphasizes its importance. Strength and courage are not optional qualities for those who follow God—they are essential. But this strength is not self-derived; it comes from the assurance that God is with us.

God's command to Joshua was accompanied by a promise: "The Lord your God will be with you wherever you go." This promise wasn't conditional on Joshua's abilities or circumstances—it was a guarantee rooted in God's unchanging character. Knowing that God's presence was with him, Joshua could step into his role with boldness and faith.

Overcoming Fear and Discouragement

Fear and discouragement often arise when we focus on our limitations or the magnitude of our challenges. Joshua 1:9 reminds us to shift our focus from what we lack to who God is. His presence transforms our perspective, giving us the courage to face even the most daunting tasks.

Courage is not about feeling fearless; it's about trusting God more than we fear the unknown. It's about taking steps of faith, even when the outcome is uncertain, and believing that God is working for our good.

Practical Steps to Live with Courage

1. **Meditate on God's Promises:**
   Reflect on verses like Joshua 1:9 to remind yourself of God's presence and faithfulness. Write them down and repeat them daily to strengthen your faith.
2. **Pray for Boldness:**
   Ask God to fill you with His strength and courage. Be specific about the fears or challenges you're facing, and invite Him to guide you through them.
3. **Take One Step at a Time:**
   Courage doesn't always require giant leaps. Start with small, faithful steps toward your goals, trusting that God will guide you each step of the way.
4. **Surround Yourself with Encouragement:**
   Lean on friends, mentors, or a faith community for support. Their prayers and encouragement can remind you of God's

promises and help you stay focused.

Living with God's Presence

The promise of God's presence is a game-changer. It assures us that we are never alone, no matter how challenging the journey may be. When we walk with Him, we carry His strength, wisdom, and peace. This awareness transforms our fears into opportunities to trust Him more deeply.

Consider the imagery of a child crossing a busy street while holding a parent's hand. The chaos and danger of the street don't disappear, but the child feels secure because they trust the one guiding them. In the same way, God's presence gives us the courage to navigate life's challenges with confidence.

A Testimony of Courage

A woman facing a career change felt overwhelmed by the uncertainty of starting over. She began meditating on Joshua 1:9, praying for God's strength and courage. As she trusted His guidance, opportunities began to open, and she found a new role that aligned with her skills and passions. Reflecting on the experience, she realized that God's promise to be with her had been the source of her boldness and peace.

Reflection on Joshua 1:9

What fears or challenges are you facing today? Write them down and place this verse beside them. Pray, "Lord, help me to be strong and courageous. Remind me of Your presence and guide me as I trust You in every step."

Walking in Strength and Courage

God's command to be strong and courageous is not a burden—it is an invitation to trust in His presence and power. Let Joshua 1:9 remind you that courage is a choice rooted in faith. No matter where life takes you, the Lord your God is with you. Step forward boldly, knowing that He is your constant guide and strength.

Chapter 24: Leaning on God for Renewal (Psalm 34:17-18)

Verse:

"The righteous cry out, and the Lord hears them; he delivers them from all their troubles. The Lord is close to the brokenhearted and saves those who are crushed in spirit."

Pain and brokenness are part of the human experience, often leaving us feeling isolated and overwhelmed. Yet, Psalm 34:17-18 offers a comforting truth: God hears our cries and draws near to us in our darkest moments. These verses remind us that no trouble is too great and no heartache too deep for God's presence and healing power.

David wrote these words from a place of personal struggle, but his testimony reveals the faithfulness of a God who listens, cares, and saves. This promise is not just for those who feel strong in their faith but also for the brokenhearted and those crushed in spirit. It is an invitation to lean on God, knowing that He is near and ready to renew.

God Hears and Responds

The first part of this passage assures us that when the righteous cry out, the Lord hears them. This is a powerful reminder that God is not distant or indifferent to our struggles. He is attentive, compassionate, and responsive. Our prayers are not lost in the void; they reach the ears of a loving Father who is ready to act.

Crying out to God requires vulnerability. It means admitting that we need His help and trusting that He will provide it. This act of surrender is often the first step toward experiencing His deliverance.

God's Nearness to the Brokenhearted

Pain has a way of making us feel alone, but this verse counters that lie with a profound truth: the Lord is close to the brokenhearted. He doesn't wait for us to have it all together before He draws near. Instead, He meets us in our brokenness, offering comfort, healing, and renewal.

Being "crushed in spirit" describes a state of deep despair, yet God promises salvation even in this place. His nearness brings hope, reminding us that He is a God who restores and redeems.

Practical Steps to Lean on God for Renewal

1. **Cry Out in Prayer:**
   Be honest with God about your pain, fears, and struggles. Share your heart with Him, knowing that He hears and cares.
2. **Meditate on His Nearness:**
   Reflect on scriptures like Psalm 34:17-18 that emphasize God's closeness. Let these verses remind you of His presence in your life.
3. **Seek Support:**
   Reach out to trusted friends, mentors, or a faith community. God often works through others to provide comfort and encouragement.
4. **Rest in His Presence:**
   Create moments of stillness to experience God's presence. Whether through worship, journaling, or quiet reflection, these moments allow His peace to fill your heart.

The Path to Renewal

Renewal begins when we acknowledge our need for God. It is a process of allowing Him to take the broken pieces of our lives and create something beautiful. This doesn't mean the pain disappears instantly, but it assures us that we are not alone in our journey.

Consider the image of a potter working with clay. When the clay becomes misshapen or broken, the potter doesn't discard it. Instead, he reshapes it, forming it into something new and purposeful. In the same way, God takes our brokenness and transforms it into something that reflects His love and grace.

A Testimony of God's Nearness

A man grieving the loss of a loved one felt crushed by the weight of his sorrow. He began praying Psalm 34:17-18 each morning, asking God to draw near. Over time, he experienced a deep sense of peace, even in the midst of his pain. Through prayer and the support of his community, he found hope and healing, discovering that God's presence truly is close to the brokenhearted.

Reflection on Psalm 34:17-18

What troubles or heartaches are you carrying today? Write them down and place this verse beside them. Pray, "Lord, I cry out to You in my brokenness. Thank You for hearing me and drawing near. Renew my heart and help me trust in Your healing power."

Walking in Renewal

Pain and heartache may feel overwhelming, but Psalm 34:17-18 reminds us that God is near, ready to deliver and heal. Let this verse guide you as you lean on Him for renewal. In every moment of brokenness, trust that He hears your cries, draws near to your heart, and restores your spirit. With God by your side, you can walk forward with hope and peace.

Chapter 25: Restoring the Soul Through Stillness (Psalm 23:2-3)

Verse:

"He makes me lie down in green pastures, he leads me beside quiet waters, he refreshes my soul. He guides me along the right paths for his name's sake."

In a world that glorifies busyness and constant activity, stillness can feel like a luxury we cannot afford. Yet, Psalm 23:2-3 reminds us of the importance of rest and renewal. God, as our Shepherd, leads us to places of peace and restoration, refreshing our souls and guiding us along paths of purpose.

These verses paint a picture of tranquility—green pastures, quiet waters, and a soul restored by the loving care of the Shepherd. This is not a temporary escape from reality but a profound invitation to experience the peace and guidance that come from being in God's presence.

The Need for Rest

Rest is not a sign of weakness; it is a divine gift. Just as a shepherd leads his sheep to safe pastures for nourishment and rest, God invites us to pause, breathe, and find renewal in Him. In our fast-paced lives, we often neglect rest, believing we must keep going to stay ahead. Yet, true restoration comes not from our efforts but from allowing God to refresh our souls.

The phrase "He makes me lie down" suggests that rest is sometimes necessary, even when we resist it. God knows our limits better than we do and lovingly calls us to slow down and find peace in His presence.

Quiet Waters for a Restored Soul

The imagery of quiet waters evokes a sense of calm and safety. Sheep, by nature, are timid creatures, and they will only drink from still waters. In the same way, our souls find refreshment in the stillness of God's presence. This stillness allows us to let go of distractions, focus on His voice, and experience the deep peace that only He can provide.

God doesn't just lead us to still waters—He restores our souls there. Restoration goes beyond physical rest; it is a renewal of the mind, heart, and spirit. It equips us to face life's challenges with clarity, strength, and purpose.

Guidance Along the Right Path

As the Shepherd, God not only restores our souls but also guides us along the right paths. His guidance is not random or aimless; it is purposeful and for His glory. When we follow His lead, we walk in alignment with His will, experiencing the peace that comes from knowing we are on the path He has prepared for us.

Practical Steps to Experience God's Restoration

1. **Schedule Time for Stillness:**
   Set aside regular moments in your day to pause and be still before God. Use this time to pray, meditate on scripture, or simply rest in His presence.
2. **Reflect on His Creation:**
   Spend time outdoors in a peaceful setting, such as a park or garden. Let the beauty of nature remind you of God's care and provision.

3. **Journal Your Thoughts:**
   Write down what's on your heart—your worries, hopes, and prayers. Journaling can help you process your thoughts and invite God into the areas where you need restoration.
4. **Practice Deep Breathing with Prayer:**
   Combine deep breathing with simple prayers, such as "Lord, restore my soul." This practice can help calm your mind and center your focus on God.

Walking in Renewal and Guidance

Restoration is not a one-time event; it is a continuous process of returning to God and allowing Him to refresh our souls. When we make time for stillness and trust in His guidance, we experience a peace that transcends the demands of daily life. This renewal empowers us to walk with purpose, knowing that our Shepherd is leading us.

A Testimony of Renewal

A young professional juggling a demanding career and personal responsibilities felt overwhelmed and burned out. She began setting aside time each evening to reflect on Psalm 23:2-3, praying for God to restore her soul. As she embraced moments of stillness and allowed God to guide her, she found renewed energy and clarity. Her workload didn't change, but her perspective did, and she experienced a peace that carried her through each day.

Reflection on Psalm 23:2-3

What areas of your life feel depleted or in need of restoration? Write them down and place this verse beside them. Pray, "Lord, lead me to Your quiet waters and refresh my soul. Help me to trust in Your guidance and rest in Your presence."

Living in the Shepherd's Care

God, as the Good Shepherd, is always leading us to places of rest and renewal. Let Psalm 23:2-3 remind you that His care is constant and His restoration is complete. Embrace His invitation to lie down in green pastures, walk beside quiet waters, and find peace in His presence. Trust His guidance as He refreshes your soul and leads you along the right paths for His name's sake.

Chapter 26: Trusting God Through Uncertainty (Proverbs 3:5-6)

Verse:

"Trust in the Lord with all your heart and lean not on your own understanding; in all your ways submit to him, and he will make your paths straight."

Uncertainty is a constant in life. Whether it's navigating career changes, health challenges, or personal decisions, the unknown often triggers stress and anxiety. Proverbs 3:5-6 offers a remedy: trust in the Lord wholeheartedly. This verse invites us to shift our focus from our limited understanding to God's infinite wisdom, submitting every aspect of our lives to His guidance.

Trusting God doesn't eliminate uncertainty, but it changes how we respond to it. Instead of striving for control or being paralyzed by fear, we can find peace in the assurance that God is directing our paths.

What It Means to Trust Wholeheartedly

Trusting God with "all your heart" means holding nothing back. It's about surrendering every worry, fear, and plan to Him, believing that He knows what's best for you. This level of trust requires faith in God's character—His goodness, wisdom, and faithfulness.

Leaning on our own understanding often leads to confusion and frustration. Our perspective is limited, shaped by emotions and incomplete information. By contrast, God's understanding is perfect, encompassing every detail of our lives. When we lean on Him, we find clarity and direction that surpass human reasoning.

Submitting Every Way to God

Submission is an act of trust. It means acknowledging that God's plan is greater than ours and inviting Him to take the lead in every area of our lives. This doesn't mean we stop making decisions or taking action; rather, it means we seek His will first and align our choices with His guidance.

The promise of this verse is profound: "He will make your paths straight." This doesn't mean the journey will always be easy, but it assures us that God is actively working to lead us in the right direction. His guidance brings purpose and peace, even in the midst of uncertainty.

Practical Steps to Trust God in Uncertainty

1. **Pray for Guidance:**
   Begin each day by asking God to direct your steps. Be specific about the areas where you need clarity, and trust that He will provide wisdom in His timing.
2. **Meditate on His Promises:**
   Reflect on verses like Proverbs 3:5-6 that affirm God's guidance. Let these truths anchor your heart when doubt creeps in.
3. **Release the Need for Control:**
   Identify areas where you're trying to control outcomes. Surrender these to God in prayer, trusting Him to work all things for your good.
4. **Celebrate Small Steps:**
   Trust often unfolds one step at a time. Recognize and thank God for the progress you see, even if the full picture isn't clear yet.

Living with Confidence in God's Plan

When we trust God with all our hearts, we experience a peace that transcends circumstances. This trust allows us to walk confidently, knowing that He is in control. Even when the path ahead seems unclear, we can move forward with the assurance that God's guidance is perfect.

Consider the imagery of a traveler navigating a dense forest. Without a map or compass, every turn feels uncertain. But with a trusted guide leading the way, the traveler can walk with confidence, trusting the guide's knowledge. In the same way, God is our guide, leading us through life's uncertainties with wisdom and care.

A Testimony of Trust

A man facing a major career decision felt overwhelmed by the options before him. He began meditating on Proverbs 3:5-6, praying for God's guidance. As he submitted his plans to the Lord, opportunities began to open that aligned with his passions and skills. Looking back, he realized that trusting God had led him to a path far better than he could have chosen on his own.

Reflection on Proverbs 3:5-6

What areas of your life feel uncertain today? Write them down and place this verse beside them. Pray, "Lord, I trust You with all my heart. Help me to let go of my own understanding and submit every aspect of my life to Your guidance. Lead me on the path You have prepared for me."

Walking in Trust

Life's uncertainties are inevitable, but Proverbs 3:5-6 reminds us that we don't have to navigate them alone. Trust in God with all your heart, lean on His wisdom, and submit your ways to Him. As you do, He will make your paths straight, guiding you with love and purpose. Walk forward with faith, knowing that the One who leads you is always trustworthy.

Chapter 27: The Strength Found in Hope (Romans 15:13)

Verse:

"May the God of hope fill you with all joy and peace as you trust in him, so that you may overflow with hope by the power of the Holy Spirit."

Hope is a powerful force. It keeps us moving forward when circumstances are tough and strengthens us when everything feels uncertain. Romans 15:13 reminds us that God is the ultimate source of hope. This hope isn't wishful thinking or fleeting optimism—it is a confident expectation rooted in God's character and promises.

Paul's prayer in this verse is a beautiful reminder that God doesn't just give us a little hope to get by. He fills us with joy and peace as we trust in Him, and this hope, fueled by the power of the Holy Spirit, overflows. It becomes more than just something we hold onto for ourselves; it spills out, inspiring and uplifting others.

God as the Source of Hope

The phrase "God of hope" emphasizes that hope is not found in our circumstances, abilities, or resources—it is found in God alone. His hope is unshakable because it is based on His unchanging nature. No matter what we face, we can trust that God's plans are good, His promises are true, and His presence is constant.

This hope is made tangible through the joy and peace that God provides. Joy is the assurance of God's goodness, and peace is the calm that comes from trusting in His control. Together, they anchor our hearts, allowing us to navigate life's challenges with confidence.

The Role of the Holy Spirit

The Holy Spirit plays a vital role in filling us with hope. As the Comforter and Helper, the Spirit works in our hearts to remind us of God's promises, guide us in truth, and strengthen our faith. The overflowing hope described in this verse is not something we manufacture on our own—it is the result of the Holy Spirit's power at work within us.

When we feel weary or discouraged, the Holy Spirit replenishes our hope, helping us to see beyond our circumstances to the bigger picture of God's plan. This hope doesn't deny the difficulties we face; it equips us to endure them with faith and resilience.

Practical Steps to Live in Overflowing Hope

1. **Anchor Yourself in Scripture:**
   Reflect on verses like Romans 15:13 that emphasize God's promises. Let His Word remind you of the hope you have in Him.
2. **Pray for Joy and Peace:**
   Ask God to fill you with the joy and peace described in this verse. Be honest about the areas where you need His hope to renew your heart.
3. **Rely on the Holy Spirit:**
   Invite the Holy Spirit to work in your life, strengthening your faith and helping you trust God more deeply. Spend time in prayer and worship to nurture this connection.
4. **Share Your Hope with Others:**
   Let the overflow of hope in your life inspire and encourage those around you. Share testimonies of God's faithfulness and be a source of light to others.

Hope That Overflows

The hope described in Romans 15:13 is not static or confined. It is dynamic and abundant, spilling over into every aspect of our lives. When we trust in God, this hope transforms how we see our circumstances and interact with the world. It fills us with confidence and courage, empowering us to face challenges and share God's love with others.

Consider the image of a cup being filled with water. When the cup is full, the water overflows, impacting everything around it. In the same way, when God fills us with hope, it overflows into our relationships, decisions, and actions, creating a ripple effect of encouragement and faith.

A Testimony of Overflowing Hope

A single mother struggling to make ends meet felt overwhelmed by the weight of her responsibilities. She began praying Romans 15:13 each morning, asking God to fill her with hope, joy, and peace. As she trusted in Him, she experienced a shift in her perspective. Though her circumstances didn't change immediately, she found renewed strength and a sense of calm. Her hope overflowed into her interactions with her children, inspiring them to trust God as well.

Reflection on Romans 15:13

What areas of your life feel devoid of hope? Write them down and place this verse beside them. Pray, "Lord, fill me with Your joy and peace as I trust in You. Let Your Spirit overflow in my life, giving me a hope that endures and inspires others."

Walking in the Power of Hope

God's hope is not limited or conditional—it is abundant and transformative. Let Romans 15:13 remind you that the God of hope is ready to fill you with joy and peace as you trust in Him. Allow the Holy

Spirit to work in your heart, producing a hope that overflows into every area of your life. No matter what challenges you face, walk forward with the confidence that your hope in God will never fail.

Chapter 28: Joy in Trials (James 1:2-3)

Verse:

"Consider it pure joy, my brothers and sisters, whenever you face trials of many kinds, because you know that the testing of your faith produces perseverance."

Trials are an inevitable part of life. Whether they come in the form of loss, disappointment, or unexpected challenges, they test our patience, faith, and resilience. James 1:2-3, however, offers a counterintuitive perspective: trials are an opportunity for joy. This passage challenges us to see difficulties not as obstacles but as pathways to growth and strength.

Joy in trials doesn't mean pretending that pain or difficulty doesn't exist. Instead, it's about recognizing the greater purpose behind the challenges we face. God uses trials to refine us, deepening our faith and building perseverance. This joy is rooted in trust, knowing that God is at work even in the hardest moments.

Reframing Trials as Opportunities

James encourages us to "consider" it pure joy when facing trials. The word "consider" suggests a deliberate choice—a decision to view trials through the lens of faith rather than fear. This perspective shift doesn't come naturally; it requires us to trust in God's wisdom and sovereignty.

Trials reveal the strength of our faith, much like fire tests and purifies gold. When we endure challenges with faith, we emerge stronger, more resilient, and more reliant on God. Perseverance, the ability to endure and remain steadfast, is a hallmark of spiritual maturity.

The Purpose Behind the Pain

The testing of faith is not meant to break us but to build us. It's through trials that we learn to depend on God, grow in patience, and develop a deeper understanding of His character. These experiences shape us into people who reflect His love, grace, and strength.

Understanding the purpose behind our trials doesn't diminish their difficulty, but it gives us hope. It assures us that our pain is not wasted and that God is using every moment to bring about His good purposes.

Practical Steps to Find Joy in Trials

1. **Pray for Perspective:**
   Ask God to help you see your trials through His eyes. Pray for the strength to trust in His plan and for the joy that comes from knowing He is with you.
2. **Focus on Growth:**
   Reflect on how past challenges have shaped you. Let these experiences remind you that God is working in your current circumstances to refine and strengthen you.
3. **Surround Yourself with Encouragement:**
   Seek out friends, mentors, or a faith community who can provide support and perspective during difficult times. Their prayers and encouragement can help you stay focused on God's promises.
4. **Celebrate Small Victories:**
   Recognize and thank God for the progress you see, even if it feels small. These moments of gratitude can shift your focus from the difficulty of the trial to the faithfulness of God.

Choosing Joy in the Midst of Pain

Joy in trials is not about denying the reality of pain but about choosing to trust God's purpose. It's about recognizing that He is using every challenge to grow us into the people He created us to be. This joy is not fleeting or dependent on circumstances—it is a deep, abiding confidence in God's goodness and faithfulness.

Consider the imagery of a tree enduring a storm. The wind may bend its branches, and the rain may strip away its leaves, but the tree's roots grow deeper as it clings to the soil. In the same way, trials deepen our faith, anchoring us more firmly in God.

A Testimony of Joy in Trials

A woman battling a prolonged health crisis found herself questioning God's plan. She began meditating on James 1:2-3, praying for the ability to see her struggle as an opportunity for growth. Over time, she noticed how her faith was deepening and her reliance on God increasing. Though her circumstances hadn't changed, her perspective had, allowing her to experience a joy that carried her through the darkest days.

Reflection on James 1:2-3

What trials are you facing today? Write them down and place this verse beside them. Pray, "Lord, help me to see my trials as opportunities for growth. Strengthen my faith and give me the joy that comes from trusting in Your plan."

Walking in Joy and Perseverance

Life's trials may test us, but they also transform us. Let James 1:2-3 remind you that God is using every challenge to produce perseverance and deepen your faith. Choose to trust Him, finding joy in the knowledge that He is with you and that your pain has a purpose. In every trial, walk forward with confidence, knowing that God is shaping you into someone who reflects His love and strength.

Chapter 29: Light in the Darkness (John 8:12)

Verse:

"When Jesus spoke again to the people, he said, 'I am the light of the world. Whoever follows me will never walk in darkness, but will have the light of life.'"

Darkness often symbolizes fear, confusion, and despair. It represents the times in life when we feel lost, unsure of our direction, or burdened by the weight of stress and anxiety. In John 8:12, Jesus declares Himself as the light of the world, offering guidance, clarity, and hope to all who follow Him. This verse is not just a statement of His identity—it is a promise to those who trust in Him.

Light has always been a powerful image of God's presence. From the pillar of fire guiding the Israelites in the wilderness to the star leading the wise men to Jesus' birthplace, light represents God's guidance and protection. In declaring Himself the light of the world, Jesus assures us that no matter how dark life feels, His light is sufficient to illuminate our path and dispel fear.

What It Means to Follow the Light

To follow Jesus as the light of the world is to trust Him as our guide. It's about walking in His truth, relying on His wisdom, and allowing His presence to lead us through life's uncertainties. This doesn't mean life will always be easy or free from challenges, but it does mean we'll never face the darkness alone.

Darkness thrives on isolation and uncertainty, but Jesus' light brings connection and clarity. When we follow Him, His light not only shows us the way forward but also reveals the beauty and purpose in the journey.

The Light of Life

The "light of life" Jesus promises is both eternal and immediate. It refers to the salvation and everlasting life He offers, as well as the guidance and peace we experience when we walk with Him daily. This light gives us the confidence to face challenges, knowing that we are never without His presence and direction.

Practical Steps to Walk in the Light

1. **Spend Time in His Word:**
   The Bible is described as a lamp to our feet and a light to our path (Psalm 119:105). Regularly reading and meditating on scripture helps us stay connected to Jesus, the source of light.
2. **Pray for Guidance:**
   In moments of confusion or fear, ask Jesus to illuminate your path. Trust that His light will guide you, even when the next step feels unclear.
3. **Reflect His Light to Others:**
   Just as the moon reflects the sun's light, we are called to reflect Jesus' light to the world. Look for opportunities to encourage, support, and share His love with those around you.
4. **Stay Close to the Source:**
   Darkness can't exist in the presence of light. The closer we stay to Jesus, the less power fear and confusion have over our lives. Cultivate a relationship with Him through worship, prayer, and fellowship.

Living in the Light

Living in Jesus' light transforms how we navigate life's challenges. Instead of stumbling through uncertainty, we walk with clarity and purpose. His light gives us confidence, peace, and the assurance that we are never alone. It also empowers us to bring hope to others, shining His light into the dark places of the world.

Imagine a lighthouse guiding a ship through a stormy sea. The light doesn't stop the waves, but it provides a beacon of hope and direction, helping the ship reach safety. In the same way, Jesus' light doesn't eliminate life's storms, but it ensures we always have a way forward.

A Testimony of Light in Darkness

A man struggling with depression felt like he was lost in darkness, unable to see a way out. He began meditating on John 8:12, asking Jesus to be his light. As he spent time in prayer and scripture, he felt a sense of clarity and hope returning to his life. Though the journey wasn't easy, he found strength in Jesus' presence, knowing that the light of the world was guiding him step by step.

Reflection on John 8:12

What areas of your life feel overshadowed by darkness? Write them down and place this verse beside them. Pray, "Lord, be the light in my darkness. Guide me with Your presence and help me to trust in Your path. Let me reflect Your light to those around me."

Walking in His Light

Jesus, the light of the world, offers a way out of darkness and into the fullness of life. Let John 8:12 remind you that His light is always available, guiding you through every challenge and uncertainty. Trust in Him, follow His lead, and let His light transform your journey.

No matter how dark the night may seem, His light is always shining, bringing hope, clarity, and peace.

Chapter 30: Strengthened by His Presence (Isaiah 41:10)

Verse:

"So do not fear, for I am with you; do not be dismayed, for I am your God. I will strengthen you and help you; I will uphold you with my righteous right hand."

Fear and dismay are natural reactions to the unknown, especially when life's challenges feel overwhelming. Isaiah 41:10 speaks directly to these emotions, offering comfort, strength, and assurance through God's presence. This verse is a powerful reminder that no matter what we face, we are never alone, and God's help is always near.

Isaiah's words are not just a call to courage—they are an invitation to trust in the unshakable character of God. His promise to strengthen, help, and uphold us is rooted in His identity as our Creator, Protector, and Provider. By focusing on His presence and power, we can move forward with confidence, even in the face of uncertainty.

The Power of God's Presence

The command "do not fear" is repeated throughout scripture, but here it is coupled with a reason: "for I am with you." God's presence is the ultimate antidote to fear. When we remember that He is by our side, we find the courage to face life's challenges with faith instead of fear.

Fear often arises when we feel alone or uncertain about what lies ahead. God's promise to be with us addresses these concerns, reminding us that His presence brings protection, guidance, and peace. He is not a distant observer—He is an active participant in our lives, walking with us every step of the way.

God's Promise to Strengthen and Uphold

The assurance "I will strengthen you and help you" highlights God's role as both a source of power and a support system. His strength is not limited by human weakness; it is infinite and perfect. When we rely on Him, we tap into a wellspring of resilience and endurance that sustains us through even the toughest trials.

The phrase "uphold you with my righteous right hand" emphasizes God's reliability and justice. His righteous right hand symbolizes His power and authority, ensuring that His promises are steadfast and unchanging. When God upholds us, we are anchored in His unshakable foundation.

Practical Steps to Trust in God's Presence

1. **Acknowledge His Presence Daily:**
   Begin each day by reminding yourself of God's promise to be with you. Pray, "Lord, thank You for Your presence. Help me to trust You in every moment."
2. **Meditate on His Strength:**
   Reflect on times when God has strengthened and helped you in the past. Let these memories reinforce your faith in His ability to do so again.
3. **Speak His Promises Aloud:**
   When fear or dismay arises, repeat Isaiah 41:10 aloud. Speaking God's Word has the power to shift your focus from fear to faith.
4. **Take Small Steps of Courage:**
   Trusting God doesn't mean eliminating all fear—it means moving forward in faith despite it. Start with small acts of

trust and build on them daily.

Living Without Fear

Fear may knock at our door, but it doesn't have to take up residence in our hearts. Isaiah 41:10 reminds us that God's presence is greater than any challenge we face. When we trust in His strength and help, we find the courage to move forward, even when the path ahead feels uncertain.

Consider the imagery of a child learning to walk while holding their parent's hand. The child may stumble or feel unsure, but the parent's steady grip provides stability and assurance. In the same way, God's righteous right hand upholds us, giving us the strength to keep going.

A Testimony of Strength and Help

A man navigating financial struggles felt overwhelmed by fear and uncertainty. He began meditating on Isaiah 41:10, praying for God's strength and help. As he trusted in God's presence, he found unexpected opportunities and support that carried him through. Reflecting on the experience, he realized that God's promise to uphold him had been his anchor during the storm.

Reflection on Isaiah 41:10

What fears or challenges are you facing today? Write them down and place this verse beside them. Pray, "Lord, thank You for Your presence. Strengthen me, help me, and uphold me with Your righteous right hand. I trust in Your power and promises."

Walking in God's Strength

Isaiah 41:10 is a beacon of hope for those facing fear or uncertainty. Let this verse remind you that God is with you, strengthening and helping you every step of the way. Trust in His presence, rely on His power, and allow Him to uphold you with His righteous hand. In every situation, walk forward with the confidence that comes from knowing you are never alone.

Chapter 31: Finding Peace in God's Timing (Ecclesiastes 3:1)

Verse:

"There is a time for everything, and a season for every activity under the heavens."

Patience can be one of the hardest virtues to cultivate, especially when life feels uncertain or when prayers seem unanswered. Ecclesiastes 3:1 reminds us that God has a plan for every moment of our lives, and His timing is always perfect. This verse offers reassurance that no season is wasted, and everything happens according to His divine purpose.

The wisdom of Ecclesiastes 3:1 challenges us to trust in God's timing, even when it doesn't align with our own. It invites us to surrender our schedules and expectations, believing that He knows what is best for us. This trust brings peace, freeing us from the stress of trying to control every detail of our lives.

The Purpose of Seasons

Life is made up of seasons—periods of joy, growth, waiting, and sometimes difficulty. Each season serves a purpose, shaping us into who God created us to be. While some seasons are filled with abundance and clarity, others may feel like a time of pruning or preparation. Trusting in God's timing means believing that every season has value, even if we don't fully understand it in the moment.

God's timing is not bound by human limitations. While we often focus on immediate results, He sees the bigger picture, orchestrating events in a way that aligns with His ultimate plan for our good.

Letting Go of Control

One of the biggest barriers to trusting God's timing is our desire for control. We want answers, results, and progress on our terms. But Ecclesiastes 3:1 calls us to relinquish that control, recognizing that God's wisdom far surpasses our own. Letting go doesn't mean passivity—it means actively trusting God while remaining faithful in the responsibilities He has given us.

When we embrace God's timing, we find peace in the waiting. Instead of rushing or resisting, we can rest in the assurance that His plans are unfolding exactly as they should.

Practical Steps to Trust God's Timing

1. **Reflect on Past Seasons:**
   Think about times in your life when God's timing proved to be perfect, even if it didn't feel that way at first. Let these experiences remind you of His faithfulness.
2. **Pray for Patience and Trust:**
   Ask God to help you trust His timing and to give you peace during seasons of waiting or uncertainty. Be honest about your struggles and invite Him to guide your perspective.
3. **Focus on the Present:**
   Instead of worrying about the future, focus on what God has placed before you today. Trust that He is preparing you for what's ahead.
4. **Meditate on His Promises:**
   Reflect on scriptures like Ecclesiastes 3:1 that emphasize God's sovereignty and timing. Let these truths anchor your heart in moments of doubt.

Peace in the Process

Trusting in God's timing doesn't eliminate the challenges of waiting, but it changes how we experience them. Instead of feeling frustrated or anxious, we can approach each season with curiosity and faith, asking, "What is God teaching me in this moment?" This mindset transforms waiting into a time of growth and preparation.

Imagine a farmer planting seeds. The farmer doesn't rush the process; he knows that growth takes time. Similarly, God's plans unfold at the right time, producing fruit that is far greater than anything we could achieve on our own.

A Testimony of Peaceful Waiting

A woman waiting to adopt a child found herself struggling with impatience and doubt. She began meditating on Ecclesiastes 3:1, praying for peace and trusting in God's timing. Over time, she realized how God was using the waiting period to prepare her heart and strengthen her faith. When the adoption finally happened, she saw how perfectly God's timing had aligned with His plans for her family.

Reflection on Ecclesiastes 3:1

What areas of your life feel uncertain or delayed? Write them down and place this verse beside them. Pray, "Lord, help me to trust in Your timing. Teach me to find peace in every season and to see Your purpose in all things."

Walking in God's Timing

Ecclesiastes 3:1 reminds us that every moment of our lives is part of God's divine plan. Let this verse encourage you to trust in His timing, even when the path forward feels unclear. Embrace each season as an opportunity for growth, knowing that His plans are always good. In every moment of waiting or uncertainty, rest in the peace that comes from trusting the One who holds time in His hands.

Chapter 32: God's Strength in Our Weakness (2 Corinthians 12:9)

Verse:

"But he said to me, 'My grace is sufficient for you, for my power is made perfect in weakness.' Therefore I will boast all the more gladly about my weaknesses, so that Christ's power may rest on me."

Weakness is something many of us try to avoid or hide. Society often views it as a flaw or failure, but in 2 Corinthians 12:9, Paul introduces a revolutionary idea: our weakness is the very space where God's power is most evident. This verse shifts the focus from self-reliance to God's all-sufficient grace, teaching us that His strength shines brightest in our most vulnerable moments.

Paul's words reflect his personal experience with a "thorn in the flesh," a struggle he repeatedly asked God to remove. Instead of taking it away, God assured him that His grace was enough. This wasn't a denial of Paul's request but a profound reminder that God's power transcends human limitations. It's a truth that invites us to lean on Him, trusting that our weaknesses are opportunities for His strength to be revealed.

God's Sufficient Grace

Grace is more than just unmerited favor—it's the sustaining power of God in our daily lives. When God says, "My grace is sufficient for you," He is promising that His provision, strength, and presence are enough to carry us through any situation. This grace doesn't eliminate our struggles, but it empowers us to endure them with peace and confidence.

Recognizing the sufficiency of God's grace requires humility. It means acknowledging that we can't do it all on our own and inviting Him to fill the gaps. This reliance transforms our perspective, allowing us to see weakness not as a barrier but as a bridge to God's power.

His Power Made Perfect

The phrase "my power is made perfect in weakness" doesn't mean that God's power is incomplete without our struggles. Rather, it highlights how His strength is fully revealed when we acknowledge our need for Him. In our weakness, His power becomes undeniable, turning our inadequacies into testimonies of His greatness.

This truth challenges the idea that we must always appear strong or self-sufficient. Instead, it frees us to embrace vulnerability, trusting that God's power is at work even when we feel inadequate.

Practical Steps to Embrace God's Strength in Weakness

1. **Acknowledge Your Weaknesses:**
   Be honest with God about the areas where you feel weak or overwhelmed. Instead of hiding them, invite Him to work through them.
2. **Pray for His Grace:**
   Ask God to sustain you with His grace in moments of difficulty. Trust that His strength is more than enough to carry you through.
3. **Celebrate God's Power:**
   Look for ways God has worked through your weaknesses in the past. Reflect on these moments as reminders of His faithfulness and power.
4. **Share Your Testimony:**
   Be open about your struggles and how God's strength has sustained you. Your story can inspire others to trust in His

power.

The Paradox of Weakness

God's kingdom often operates on principles that seem counterintuitive. Strength through weakness is one such paradox. When we stop striving to appear strong and allow God to take control, we experience a freedom and peace that can only come from Him. His power turns our struggles into platforms for His glory, reminding us that our worth is not dependent on our abilities but on His presence in our lives.

Consider the imagery of a broken vessel. Though it may seem flawed, the cracks allow light to shine through, illuminating everything around it. In the same way, our weaknesses allow God's light to shine more brightly, drawing others to His love and grace.

A Testimony of Strength in Weakness

A man struggling with anxiety felt paralyzed by his inability to control his thoughts. He began praying 2 Corinthians 12:9 daily, asking God to show His strength in his weakness. Over time, he experienced a shift—not because the anxiety disappeared, but because he learned to lean on God's grace. His vulnerability became a source of strength, inspiring others who faced similar struggles to trust in God's power.

Reflection on 2 Corinthians 12:9

What weaknesses are you wrestling with today? Write them down and place this verse beside them. Pray, "Lord, I surrender my weaknesses to You. Let Your grace sustain me and Your power work through me. Help me to trust in Your sufficiency."

Walking in His Strength

Weakness is not a limitation—it's an opportunity for God to demonstrate His power. Let 2 Corinthians 12:9 remind you that His grace is sufficient for every challenge you face. Embrace your limitations as invitations for His strength, and trust that His power is made perfect in your weakness. Walk forward with confidence, knowing that His grace will sustain you and His power will carry you through.

Chapter 33: Anchored in Hope (Hebrews 6:19)

Verse:

"We have this hope as an anchor for the soul, firm and secure. It enters the inner sanctuary behind the curtain."

Hope is essential for navigating life's uncertainties. It steadies us in the face of challenges and keeps us moving forward when circumstances threaten to overwhelm us. Hebrews 6:19 describes this hope as an anchor for the soul, offering a powerful image of stability and security. This anchor is not based on fleeting emotions or worldly assurances but is rooted in the unchanging promises of God.

The context of this verse speaks to the faithfulness of God's covenant and His unwavering commitment to His people. Just as an anchor holds a ship steady in rough waters, our hope in God keeps us grounded, no matter what storms we face. This hope is not only firm but also secure, giving us the confidence to trust in God's plan and timing.

The Nature of Hope as an Anchor

An anchor provides stability by holding a vessel in place, preventing it from drifting or being swept away by strong currents. Similarly, the hope we have in Christ keeps us steady when life feels chaotic. This hope is not wishful thinking; it is a confident expectation based on the truth of God's Word.

The phrase "firm and secure" emphasizes the unshakable nature of this hope. It is not dependent on circumstances but on the character of

God, who is faithful and unchanging. When we place our trust in Him, we find a foundation that cannot be moved.

Hope That Enters the Inner Sanctuary

The reference to the "inner sanctuary behind the curtain" points to the holy place within the temple, symbolizing God's presence. Through Christ, our hope is anchored in the very presence of God, giving us access to His guidance, peace, and strength. This connection is both intimate and powerful, assuring us that we are never alone in our struggles.

Practical Steps to Stay Anchored in Hope

1. **Cling to God's Promises:**
   Spend time reading and meditating on scriptures that affirm God's faithfulness. Let these promises remind you of the hope you have in Him.
2. **Pray for Steadiness:**
   In moments of uncertainty or fear, ask God to anchor your heart in His truth. Trust that His presence will keep you steady.
3. **Celebrate God's Faithfulness:**
   Reflect on how God has been faithful in the past. Let these memories strengthen your hope for the future.
4. **Encourage Others with Hope:**
   Share your testimony of God's faithfulness with those who are struggling. Your story can inspire others to anchor their hope in Him as well.

Living with an Anchored Soul

A life anchored in hope is not free from storms, but it is marked by peace and resilience. When we trust in God's promises, we find the strength to face challenges with confidence, knowing that He is in control. This hope gives us the courage to persevere and the assurance that our future is secure in His hands.

Consider the imagery of a ship during a storm. The waves may batter it, and the winds may howl, but the anchor keeps it from being carried away. In the same way, our hope in God holds us steady, allowing us to endure life's challenges with faith and confidence.

A Testimony of Anchored Hope

A woman facing the uncertainty of a major life transition felt overwhelmed by fear of the unknown. She began meditating on Hebrews 6:19, reminding herself daily that her hope was anchored in God's promises. As she prayed and reflected, she found peace and clarity, trusting that God's presence would guide her through. Her confidence became a testimony to those around her, inspiring others to place their hope in Him.

Reflection on Hebrews 6:19

What areas of your life feel uncertain or unsteady today? Write them down and place this verse beside them. Pray, "Lord, thank You for the hope that anchors my soul. Help me to trust in Your promises and remain steady in Your presence, no matter what challenges I face."

Walking in Hope That Anchors

Hope in God is not just a concept—it is a stabilizing force that sustains us through life's challenges. Let Hebrews 6:19 remind you that this hope is firm, secure, and rooted in God's presence. Trust in His promises, and allow His hope to anchor your soul, keeping you steady and secure through every storm. With your heart anchored in Him, you can face any uncertainty with confidence and peace.

Chapter 34: Faithful in Every Season (Lamentations 3:22-23)

Verse:

"Because of the Lord's great love we are not consumed, for his compassions never fail. They are new every morning; great is your faithfulness."

Life often feels like a series of unpredictable seasons, with moments of joy and sorrow, clarity and confusion, triumph and struggle. In the midst of this, Lamentations 3:22-23 reminds us of the constancy of God's love and faithfulness. No matter what season we find ourselves in, His compassion sustains us, and His faithfulness renews us every day.

These verses were written during a time of deep sorrow and hardship for the people of Israel. Yet, even in the midst of despair, the author declares the unwavering love and mercy of God. This powerful truth encourages us to trust in His presence and provision, regardless of our circumstances.

God's Unfailing Compassion

The phrase "because of the Lord's great love we are not consumed" speaks to the protective and sustaining nature of God's compassion. His love is not fleeting or conditional—it is steadfast and unchanging. No matter how overwhelming our circumstances may feel, His mercy ensures that we are not overtaken by them.

God's compassion is deeply personal. He sees our struggles, knows our needs, and responds with love and care. His mercy meets us in our weakest moments, reminding us that we are never beyond the reach of His grace.

New Every Morning

The idea that God's compassions are "new every morning" emphasizes His daily provision. Each day comes with its own challenges, but God's mercy is always sufficient to meet our needs. This renewal reflects His faithfulness, assuring us that He will provide fresh strength, peace, and guidance for every moment.

This truth invites us to approach each day with hope, trusting that God's presence and power are with us. No matter how difficult yesterday may have been, today is an opportunity to experience His mercies anew.

Great Is Your Faithfulness

The declaration "great is your faithfulness" is a profound reminder of God's reliability. His faithfulness is not dependent on our actions or circumstances—it is rooted in His character. When life feels uncertain, we can anchor ourselves in the knowledge that God is always true to His promises.

God's faithfulness extends to every aspect of our lives, from the smallest details to the greatest challenges. He never changes, and His love for us never wavers. This assurance gives us the confidence to trust Him in every season.

Practical Steps to Rest in God's Faithfulness

1. **Begin Each Day with Gratitude:**
   Take a moment each morning to thank God for His new mercies. Reflect on how His faithfulness has sustained you.
2. **Meditate on His Promises:**

Spend time reading scriptures that highlight God's faithfulness, such as Lamentations 3:22-23. Let these verses remind you of His unwavering love.

3. **Trust Him in the Present Moment:**
   When challenges arise, remind yourself that God's mercy is sufficient for today. Focus on His presence and trust Him to guide you.
4. **Share His Faithfulness with Others:**
   Encourage those around you by sharing how God's love and mercy have impacted your life. Your testimony can inspire others to trust in His faithfulness.

Living with Confidence in God's Love

God's faithfulness is the foundation of our hope and peace. When we trust in His love and mercy, we can face each day with confidence, knowing that He is with us. This trust transforms how we navigate life's seasons, allowing us to experience His joy and peace even in the midst of challenges.

Consider the imagery of a sunrise. Each morning, the light breaks through the darkness, signaling the start of a new day. In the same way, God's mercies renew our hearts, bringing hope and clarity no matter what the previous day held.

A Testimony of Faithfulness

A woman facing financial struggles felt overwhelmed by worry and fear. She began meditating on Lamentations 3:22-23, praying for God's mercy to renew her each day. As she trusted in His faithfulness, she saw unexpected opportunities and provision unfold. Looking back, she realized that His compassion had sustained her through the hardest moments.

Reflection on Lamentations 3:22-23

What challenges are you facing today? Write them down and place this verse beside them. Pray, "Lord, thank You for Your great love and mercy. Help me to trust in Your faithfulness and to rest in the assurance of Your compassion."

Walking in His Faithfulness

Life's seasons may change, but God's love and mercy remain constant. Let Lamentations 3:22-23 remind you that His compassion is always sufficient, His faithfulness is unshakable, and His mercies are new every morning. Trust in His presence, lean on His love, and walk forward with confidence, knowing that He is with you in every moment.

Chapter 35: Peace Beyond Understanding (Philippians 4:7)

Verse:

"And the peace of God, which transcends all understanding, will guard your hearts and your minds in Christ Jesus."

In a world filled with uncertainty, the idea of experiencing peace can often feel elusive. Philippians 4:7 offers a profound promise: God's peace, which surpasses human comprehension, will protect both our hearts and minds. This peace is not tied to our circumstances but is rooted in the presence of Christ, offering calm and assurance even in the midst of life's storms.

Paul wrote these words while imprisoned, facing an uncertain future. Yet, his confidence in God's peace was unwavering. This verse serves as a reminder that true peace is not the absence of conflict or difficulty—it is the presence of God, anchoring us in His love and sovereignty.

The Nature of God's Peace

The peace of God is unlike anything the world can offer. It is not dependent on external conditions but flows from a deep trust in His character and promises. This peace transcends understanding, meaning it goes beyond logic or explanation. It steadies us when circumstances seem overwhelming and assures us of God's presence and provision.

God's peace doesn't ignore reality—it meets us in the midst of it. It calms our fears, quiets our anxieties, and allows us to rest in the assurance that He is in control.

Guarding Our Hearts and Minds

Paul uses the imagery of a guard to describe the protective nature of God's peace. Just as a guard protects a city from threats, God's peace shields our hearts and minds from the worries and fears that seek to overwhelm us. This protection is not passive; it is active and powerful, ensuring that our thoughts and emotions remain anchored in Christ.

The heart represents our emotions, and the mind represents our thoughts. When God's peace guards both, we experience a wholeness that enables us to navigate life's challenges with confidence and clarity.

Practical Steps to Embrace God's Peace

1. **Pray with Thanksgiving:**
   Before this verse, Philippians 4:6 encourages us to bring our requests to God with thanksgiving. Gratitude shifts our focus from what we lack to what God has already provided, opening the door for His peace.
2. **Meditate on His Promises:**
   Reflect on scriptures that affirm God's presence and sovereignty. Let these truths replace anxious thoughts with a sense of calm and assurance.
3. **Surrender Control:**
   Acknowledge the areas of your life where you're trying to hold control. Release these to God in prayer, trusting Him to handle them.
4. **Practice Mindfulness in Christ:**
   Focus on being present with God. Whether through prayer, worship, or quiet reflection, allow His presence to fill your heart and mind with peace.

Living in Peace That Transcends

Living in God's peace doesn't mean life will be free from challenges. It means that we can face those challenges with a calm assurance that God is with us and for us. This peace transforms how we respond to difficulties, enabling us to trust Him even when the path ahead is unclear.

Consider the imagery of a calm harbor during a storm. The waters beyond may be rough, but the harbor remains undisturbed. In the same way, God's peace provides a safe haven for our hearts and minds, allowing us to rest in His presence no matter what storms we face.

A Testimony of Peace

A man struggling with overwhelming job stress felt his anxiety building daily. He began meditating on Philippians 4:7, praying for God's peace to guard his heart and mind. As he prayed and focused on God's promises, he noticed a shift. His circumstances didn't change immediately, but his perspective did. He found strength and calm to face each day, confident that God's peace would sustain him.

Reflection on Philippians 4:7

What areas of your life feel overwhelming today? Write them down and place this verse beside them. Pray, "Lord, let Your peace guard my heart and mind. Help me to trust in Your presence and rest in the assurance of Your love."

Walking in His Peace

God's peace is a gift that transcends understanding, protecting us from the anxieties and fears that threaten to overwhelm us. Let Philippians 4:7 remind you that this peace is always available through Christ. Trust in His presence, release your worries to Him, and allow His peace to guard your heart and mind. No matter what challenges you face, walk forward with the calm assurance that His peace is greater than any storm.

Chapter 36: Strength in Stillness (Exodus 14:14)

Verse:

"The Lord will fight for you; you need only to be still."

In the midst of life's battles, our instinct is often to act, fix, or control. Yet, Exodus 14:14 delivers a counterintuitive message: be still. These words were spoken to the Israelites as they faced the seemingly impossible—Pharaoh's army behind them and the Red Sea before them. Fearful and unsure, they were commanded to trust in God's power rather than their own abilities. This verse serves as a powerful reminder that stillness is not passivity; it is an active choice to trust God to fight on our behalf.

The Context of Stillness

The Israelites' situation was dire. They were trapped, and escape seemed impossible. Moses' command to "be still" might have seemed irrational, but it was rooted in faith. God's ability to deliver them didn't depend on their strength or strategies—it rested solely on His power and plan. This moment was an invitation for them to trust fully in His sovereignty.

Stillness, in this context, is not about doing nothing; it's about relinquishing the illusion of control and placing complete trust in God. It's a posture of faith that acknowledges, "I can't, but God can."

The Lord Will Fight for You

The promise "The Lord will fight for you" reflects God's role as a protector and deliverer. Throughout scripture, we see examples of His intervention, often in ways that defy human understanding. When we trust Him to fight for us, we are reminded that the battle belongs to Him, not us.

This doesn't mean we won't face challenges or feel the weight of the battle. It means we don't have to carry it alone. God's presence assures us that we are not abandoned or powerless—He is actively working on our behalf.

Practical Steps to Embrace Stillness and Trust

1. **Pause and Pray:**
   In moments of fear or stress, take a moment to pause and pray. Acknowledge God's presence and ask for His guidance and intervention.
2. **Surrender the Outcome:**
   Identify the battles you're trying to fight on your own. Write them down and symbolically release them to God in prayer, trusting Him to take control.
3. **Meditate on God's Faithfulness:**
   Reflect on times when God has fought for you in the past. Let these memories strengthen your faith in His ability to deliver you again.
4. **Practice Physical Stillness:**
   Spend time in quiet reflection, focusing on God's promises. Use this time to rest in His presence and allow His peace to fill your heart.

Finding Strength in Stillness

Stillness is not a lack of action; it is a deliberate choice to trust in God's power over our own efforts. It requires humility and faith, reminding us that His ways are higher than ours. When we rest in His presence, we find strength, clarity, and peace to face the challenges before us.

Imagine a soldier in a fortified tower, watching as reinforcements arrive to secure the battlefield. The soldier's role is not to fight alone but to trust in the strength of those who have come to protect and deliver. In the same way, our role is to trust in God, knowing that He is fighting for us.

A Testimony of Stillness

A man facing a legal battle felt overwhelmed by the complexity and uncertainty of the situation. He began meditating on Exodus 14:14, reminding himself that the Lord would fight for him. As he released his fears to God and chose stillness over striving, he experienced a peace that carried him through the process. In the end, the resolution came in ways he could not have anticipated, confirming God's faithfulness.

Reflection on Exodus 14:14

What battles are you facing today? Write them down and place this verse beside them. Pray, "Lord, I trust You to fight for me. Help me to release control and rest in Your strength. Teach me to be still and to trust in Your plan."

Walking in Trust and Stillness

Exodus 14:14 reminds us that stillness is a powerful expression of faith. Let this verse encourage you to trust in God's power to fight for you. Be still in His presence, release your fears to Him, and allow His strength to sustain you. No matter how overwhelming the battle may seem, trust that He is working on your behalf, leading you toward victory.

Chapter 37: Faith That Moves Mountains (Matthew 17:20)

Verse:

"He replied, 'Because you have so little faith. Truly I tell you, if you have faith as small as a mustard seed, you can say to this mountain, "Move from here to there," and it will move. Nothing will be impossible for you.'"

Faith is one of the most powerful forces in the life of a believer. In Matthew 17:20, Jesus speaks to the transformative potential of even the smallest amount of faith. He compares it to a mustard seed—a tiny seed that grows into one of the largest garden plants, symbolizing how faith, no matter how small, can yield incredible results when placed in the hands of God.

This verse isn't about the size of our faith but the greatness of the One in whom our faith is placed. It challenges us to trust God with the "mountains" in our lives—those obstacles that seem immovable—and to believe in His ability to do the impossible.

The Power of Mustard-Seed Faith

The mustard seed is one of the smallest seeds, yet it holds the potential for remarkable growth. Jesus uses this imagery to emphasize that faith doesn't have to be enormous to be effective. Even a small amount of genuine faith, when rooted in God, can produce extraordinary results.

This truth is both encouraging and challenging. It reminds us that the effectiveness of our faith is not determined by its size but by its sincerity. When we trust God with even the smallest seed of faith, He can accomplish far more than we could imagine.

Mountains as Metaphors

The "mountains" in this verse represent the seemingly insurmountable challenges we face. These could be obstacles in our relationships, finances, health, or spiritual growth. Jesus' words remind us that no challenge is too great for God. Faith doesn't deny the difficulty of the mountain but trusts in God's ability to move it.

Moving a mountain requires perseverance, trust, and action. It calls us to partner with God, stepping forward in faith even when the path ahead seems impossible.

Practical Steps to Grow and Apply Faith

1. **Start Small:**
   Begin by trusting God with small areas of your life. As you see His faithfulness, your faith will grow stronger.
2. **Speak to Your Mountains:**
   Identify the challenges in your life and pray specifically for God to move them. Speak His promises over these situations, trusting in His power.
3. **Nurture Your Faith:**
   Like a mustard seed, faith grows when it is nurtured. Spend time in prayer, worship, and scripture to strengthen your trust in God.
4. **Take Faithful Steps:**
   Faith often requires action. Ask God to show you the next step, and move forward with confidence, knowing He is with you.

Trusting the God of the Impossible

Jesus' promise in Matthew 17:20 challenges us to see beyond our limitations and trust in God's unlimited power. When we place our faith in Him, we align ourselves with His purposes, allowing Him to work in and through us. This doesn't mean every mountain will be removed immediately, but it assures us that God is actively working for our good.

Imagine a hiker standing at the base of a massive mountain. From their perspective, it seems impossible to climb or move. But with the right tools and guidance, the mountain becomes navigable. In the same way, faith equips us to face life's challenges with the assurance that God is leading us to victory.

A Testimony of Moving Mountains

A woman struggling with overwhelming debt felt hopeless about her situation. She began praying Matthew 17:20 daily, asking God for the faith to overcome her financial challenges. As she trusted Him and took small, faithful steps—budgeting, seeking counsel, and applying for new opportunities—she began to see progress. Over time, her "mountain" moved, and she experienced God's provision in ways she never imagined.

Reflection on Matthew 17:20

What mountains are you facing today? Write them down and place this verse beside them. Pray, "Lord, I trust You to move the mountains in my life. Strengthen my faith and help me to walk forward with confidence, knowing that nothing is impossible for You."

Walking in Faith That Moves Mountains

Matthew 17:20 reminds us that even the smallest amount of faith, when placed in God, can accomplish incredible things. Let this verse inspire you to trust Him with the challenges in your life, no matter how daunting they may seem. Speak to your mountains, nurture your faith, and step forward with confidence. With God, nothing is impossible, and every mountain can be moved.

Chapter 38: Renewed Strength in Waiting (Isaiah 40:31)

Verse:

"But those who hope in the Lord will renew their strength. They will soar on wings like eagles; they will run and not grow weary, they will walk and not be faint."

Waiting can feel like one of the hardest things to do. In a fast-paced world, patience often feels like a burden rather than a virtue. Yet Isaiah 40:31 reminds us that waiting on the Lord is not passive—it is an active expression of trust that leads to renewed strength and resilience. This verse offers hope to anyone feeling weary or discouraged, promising that God's strength will sustain and empower them.

Isaiah uses vivid imagery to describe the transformation that comes from waiting on God. From soaring like eagles to running without weariness and walking without fainting, this verse emphasizes the spiritual, emotional, and physical renewal that flows from placing our hope in Him.

What It Means to Hope in the Lord

Hoping in the Lord is not merely wishing for better circumstances; it is a confident expectation rooted in His character and promises. It requires surrendering our timelines and trusting that God's plan is unfolding perfectly, even when we can't see the full picture.

This hope is not idle; it is an active dependence on God that involves prayer, worship, and obedience. When we place our hope in Him, we shift our focus from our limitations to His infinite power and grace.

Renewed Strength for Every Season

The promise of renewed strength is central to this verse. Life's challenges can drain us, leaving us feeling depleted and unable to move forward. But when we wait on the Lord, He replenishes what stress, fear, and fatigue have taken. This renewal is not just physical—it encompasses our mind, heart, and spirit, equipping us to face each day with confidence and peace.

Isaiah's imagery captures three distinct forms of strength:

1. **Soaring on Wings Like Eagles:**
   There are moments when God lifts us above our circumstances, giving us a perspective that transcends the chaos below. Like eagles gliding on air currents, we are carried by His power, free from striving.
2. **Running Without Weariness:**
   At times, we need endurance to press forward through challenges. God's strength enables us to run the race with perseverance, sustaining us when we feel like giving up.
3. **Walking Without Fainting:**
   In quieter seasons, God gives us the strength to take steady steps forward. Even when progress feels slow, His presence ensures we do not falter.

Practical Steps to Wait on the Lord

1. **Cultivate Stillness:**
   Set aside time each day to be still before God. Use this time to pray, meditate on scripture, and listen for His voice.
2. **Focus on His Promises:**
   Reflect on verses like Isaiah 40:31 that affirm God's faithfulness. Let these promises anchor your hope during

difficult seasons.

3. **Embrace Community:**
   Surround yourself with people who encourage your faith. Their prayers and support can help you stay focused on God's strength.
4. **Celebrate Small Victories:**
   Recognize the ways God is renewing your strength, even in small ways. Gratitude fosters hope and keeps you moving forward.

Living with Renewed Strength

Waiting on the Lord transforms how we navigate life's challenges. Instead of relying on our own strength, we draw from His unlimited resources. This trust brings peace, resilience, and the confidence to face each day knowing that He is with us.

Consider the imagery of a marathon runner. Without proper training and nourishment, a runner quickly grows weary. But with the right preparation and support, they can endure to the finish line. In the same way, waiting on the Lord renews our strength, enabling us to run life's race with endurance and joy.

A Testimony of Renewed Strength

A woman balancing work, family, and health challenges felt completely drained. She began meditating on Isaiah 40:31, praying for God's strength to carry her through. As she focused on waiting on Him—through prayer, worship, and intentional rest—she experienced a profound renewal. Her circumstances didn't change overnight, but her perspective and energy did, allowing her to move forward with hope and resilience.

Reflection on Isaiah 40:31

What areas of your life feel exhausting today? Write them down and place this verse beside them. Pray, "Lord, help me to wait on You. Renew my strength and teach me to trust in Your timing and plan."

Walking in Renewed Strength

Isaiah 40:31 reminds us that waiting on the Lord is not a burden but a blessing. Let this verse encourage you to trust in His promises, rest in His presence, and draw strength from His power. Whether you need to soar, run, or walk, His strength is sufficient for every season. Move forward with confidence, knowing that God is renewing you day by day.

Chapter 39: Casting Your Cares on Him (1 Peter 5:7)

Verse:

"Cast all your anxiety on him because he cares for you."

Anxiety can feel like a heavy weight, pulling us down and consuming our thoughts. In 1 Peter 5:7, we are invited to cast our cares on God, not because He is obligated, but because He genuinely cares for us. This verse is a reminder that we don't have to carry our burdens alone—God is ready and willing to shoulder them for us.

Peter's words are not a superficial solution to anxiety. They offer a profound truth: when we entrust our worries to God, we experience His peace and provision in ways that transform how we face life's challenges. Casting our cares on Him is an act of faith, a declaration that we trust His ability to handle what feels overwhelming to us.

What It Means to Cast Your Anxiety

The word "cast" implies an intentional action. It means throwing or placing something with purpose. Casting our anxiety on God involves actively giving Him our worries, fears, and uncertainties. It's not about ignoring our problems but surrendering them to the One who has the power to resolve them.

This process requires humility, as Peter writes in the preceding verse: "Humble yourselves, therefore, under God's mighty hand." Acknowledging that we need God's help is the first step in experiencing His care and provision.

Because He Cares for You

The assurance "because he cares for you" is deeply personal. God's care is not abstract or distant—it is intimate and specific. He knows every detail of our lives, every fear we hold, and every burden we carry. His love compels Him to respond with compassion and provision.

This truth reminds us that we are never alone. No matter how isolated or overwhelmed we feel, God is always present, ready to carry our burdens and provide the strength we need.

Practical Steps to Cast Your Cares on God

1. **Name Your Worries:**
   Take time to identify the specific anxieties weighing on your heart. Write them down as a way of acknowledging them before God.
2. **Pray with Honesty:**
   Bring your worries to God in prayer. Be honest about your fears and ask Him to take them from you. Trust that He hears and cares.
3. **Release Control:**
   Surrender the outcome to God. Remind yourself that He is in control and that His plans are better than anything you could orchestrate on your own.
4. **Replace Worry with Truth:**
   Meditate on scriptures like 1 Peter 5:7 that affirm God's care. Let His Word replace anxious thoughts with peace and assurance.

Living Free from Anxiety's Grip

Casting our cares on God doesn't mean we'll never feel anxious again, but it transforms how we respond to those feelings. Instead of being consumed by worry, we learn to trust God with the things we cannot control. This trust brings peace, allowing us to focus on what He has called us to do.

Consider the imagery of a hiker with a heavy backpack. As they travel, the weight becomes unbearable. But when they hand the backpack to someone stronger, they can move forward with freedom and ease. In the same way, God invites us to give Him our burdens, freeing us to walk in His peace and strength.

A Testimony of Casting Cares

A man struggling with financial uncertainty found himself consumed by anxiety. He began meditating on 1 Peter 5:7, praying daily for God to take his worries. As he trusted God with his situation, he experienced a sense of peace and clarity. Over time, he saw how God provided in unexpected ways, confirming that casting his cares on the Lord was the right choice.

Reflection on 1 Peter 5:7

What anxieties are you carrying today? Write them down and place this verse beside them. Pray, "Lord, I cast my cares on You. Help me to trust in Your care and to release the burdens that I cannot carry alone."

Walking in His Care

1 Peter 5:7 reminds us that God's care is always available. Let this verse encourage you to release your anxieties to Him, trusting that He is both willing and able to carry them. Cast your cares on Him and walk forward in freedom, knowing that His love and provision are more than enough for every challenge you face.

Chapter 40: Perfect Love Casts Out Fear (1 John 4:18)

Verse:

"There is no fear in love. But perfect love drives out fear, because fear has to do with punishment. The one who fears is not made perfect in love."

Fear is a powerful emotion that often holds us back, clouds our judgment, and robs us of peace. In 1 John 4:18, we are reminded that fear has no place in the presence of God's perfect love. This verse offers both a challenge and a comfort: as we grow in our understanding of God's love, fear loses its grip on our hearts.

John contrasts fear with love, emphasizing that fear stems from an expectation of punishment or harm. In Christ, we are set free from condemnation, allowing us to live without fear. God's perfect love provides safety, assurance, and confidence, enabling us to face life's uncertainties with peace and courage.

Understanding Perfect Love

Perfect love is not based on human efforts or emotions—it is the unconditional, unchanging love of God. This love is fully expressed through Jesus, who bore the punishment for our sins and reconciled us to God. When we accept His love, we are freed from the fear of judgment and empowered to live in the security of His grace.

God's perfect love is not just about what He has done but also about who He is. His love is patient, kind, and steadfast, never failing even when we fall short. This love transforms us, reshaping how we see ourselves, others, and the challenges we face.

Driving Out Fear

Fear thrives on uncertainty and the unknown, but God's love brings clarity and peace. The more we immerse ourselves in His love, the less power fear has over us. This doesn't mean we'll never feel afraid, but it assures us that fear no longer controls us.

Perfect love drives out fear because it reassures us of our identity in Christ. We are beloved children of God, fully accepted and cared for. This truth gives us the confidence to face life with boldness, knowing that nothing can separate us from His love.

Practical Steps to Live in God's Perfect Love

1. **Meditate on God's Love:**
   Reflect on scriptures that describe God's love, such as 1 Corinthians 13:4-8 and Romans 8:38-39. Let these verses remind you of His unwavering commitment to you.
2. **Speak Truth Over Fear:**
   When fear arises, counter it with the truth of God's love. Declare verses like 1 John 4:18 aloud, reminding yourself that His perfect love drives out fear.
3. **Pray for a Deeper Understanding:**
   Ask God to reveal His love to you in new and profound ways. Trust that as you grow in your understanding of His love, fear will diminish.
4. **Act in Love:**
   Step out in faith to love others as God loves you. Serving and caring for others shifts your focus from fear to the power of love at work in your life.

Freedom Through Love

Living in God's perfect love doesn't mean we'll never face challenges, but it assures us that we are never alone. His love provides the foundation for courage, resilience, and peace, allowing us to walk forward with confidence. As we rest in His love, fear loses its hold, and we experience the freedom that comes from being fully known and fully loved.

Consider the imagery of a child running into their parent's arms during a thunderstorm. The storm doesn't stop, but the child feels safe because they are held by someone who loves and protects them. In the same way, God's perfect love shelters us, driving out the fears that threaten to overwhelm us.

A Testimony of Love Over Fear

A man battling fear of failure felt paralyzed by the weight of expectations. He began meditating on 1 John 4:18, praying for God's love to replace his fears. As he spent time in scripture and prayer, he experienced a shift. Fear no longer dictated his decisions, and he found the courage to step into new opportunities with confidence. God's love had transformed his perspective, freeing him from the chains of fear.

Reflection on 1 John 4:18

What fears are holding you back today? Write them down and place this verse beside them. Pray, "Lord, let Your perfect love cast out my fear. Help me to trust in Your love and to walk in the freedom You have given me."

Walking in Perfect Love

1 John 4:18 reminds us that fear has no place in the presence of God's love. Let this verse encourage you to embrace His perfect love, allowing it to drive out fear and bring peace to your heart. Trust in His love, rest in His grace, and live with the confidence that comes from being fully

loved by Him. Walk forward in freedom, knowing that His perfect love is greater than any fear you face.

Chapter 41: The Strength of God's Joy (Nehemiah 8:10)

Verse:

"Do not grieve, for the joy of the Lord is your strength."

Life is full of moments that test our resolve—times of loss, uncertainty, or overwhelming responsibility. In Nehemiah 8:10, we are reminded that the joy of the Lord is not just a feeling but a source of strength. This joy, rooted in God's presence and promises, empowers us to face life's challenges with resilience and hope.

This verse was spoken during a time of renewal for the Israelites. As they listened to God's law, they were convicted of their sins and began to weep. But Nehemiah encouraged them to rejoice, reminding them that God's joy was their strength. This call to joy was not a dismissal of their emotions but an invitation to embrace the hope and restoration that comes from God.

What Is the Joy of the Lord?

The joy of the Lord is not dependent on circumstances; it is a deep and abiding sense of peace and confidence that comes from knowing God. This joy is grounded in His character—His faithfulness, goodness, and love. It is the assurance that, no matter what we face, He is with us, for us, and working all things for our good.

This joy is not fleeting or superficial. It sustains us through trials, giving us the strength to persevere and the courage to trust in God's plan. It is a wellspring of hope that flows from our relationship with Him, renewing our hearts and minds daily.

Joy as a Source of Strength

When we rely on our own strength, we quickly become weary. But when we draw from the joy of the Lord, we tap into a limitless source of energy and resilience. This joy doesn't ignore the reality of pain or difficulty—it exists alongside it, reminding us that God's presence and promises are greater than our struggles.

Joy transforms how we approach challenges. It shifts our perspective from defeat to victory, from fear to faith. It reminds us that our strength comes not from our circumstances but from our connection to the One who holds all things together.

Practical Steps to Experience the Joy of the Lord

1. **Spend Time in God's Presence:**
   Joy is a byproduct of intimacy with God. Make time for prayer, worship, and reflection to deepen your relationship with Him.
2. **Reflect on His Faithfulness:**
   Remember the ways God has been faithful in your life. Let these memories fill you with gratitude and renew your joy.
3. **Choose Gratitude:**
   Joy grows when we focus on what we have rather than what we lack. Practice daily gratitude, thanking God for His blessings and provision.
4. **Serve Others:**
   Sharing God's love with others can reignite your joy. Look for opportunities to encourage, support, and bless those around you.

Living in God's Strength

When we embrace the joy of the Lord, we find a strength that transcends human understanding. This joy equips us to face life's challenges with courage and peace, knowing that God is our refuge and source of hope. It empowers us to live with confidence, trusting that His grace is sufficient for every need.

Consider the imagery of a tree planted by a stream. Its roots draw nourishment from the water, allowing it to remain strong and vibrant even in times of drought. In the same way, the joy of the Lord sustains us, providing strength and stability no matter what we face.

A Testimony of Joy and Strength

A woman grieving the loss of a loved one felt overwhelmed by sorrow. She began meditating on Nehemiah 8:10, praying for God's joy to sustain her. As she spent time in worship and reflected on His promises, she experienced a peace that carried her through her grief. Though her circumstances didn't change, her heart was renewed, and she found the strength to move forward with hope.

Reflection on Nehemiah 8:10

What challenges are you facing today that feel overwhelming? Write them down and place this verse beside them. Pray, "Lord, let Your joy be my strength. Renew my heart and help me to trust in Your presence and promises."

Walking in the Joy of the Lord

Nehemiah 8:10 reminds us that God's joy is a powerful source of strength. Let this verse encourage you to embrace His joy, allowing it to sustain and renew you. Trust in His presence, rest in His promises, and draw strength from the unshakable joy that comes from knowing Him. Walk forward with confidence, knowing that His joy will carry you through every season.

Chapter 42: A Peaceful Mindset (Romans 8:6)

Verse:

"The mind governed by the flesh is death, but the mind governed by the Spirit is life and peace."

Our mindset shapes how we experience the world. Romans 8:6 highlights the stark contrast between a mind focused on worldly desires and one led by the Spirit of God. A mindset governed by the flesh leads to spiritual stagnation and disconnection from God, while a Spirit-led mindset brings life and peace. This verse invites us to align our thoughts with God's truth, allowing His Spirit to guide and transform us.

Paul's words remind us that peace is not just an emotion—it's a state of being rooted in our relationship with God. When we allow the Holy Spirit to govern our thoughts, we experience a profound sense of wholeness and purpose that transcends our circumstances.

The Danger of a Flesh-Governed Mind

The "flesh" refers to our human nature apart from God—our tendency to prioritize selfish desires, fear, and control over faith and obedience. A mind governed by the flesh is consumed by worry, pride, and the pursuit of things that ultimately cannot satisfy. This mindset leads to spiritual death, separating us from the fullness of life that God intends for us.

When we focus solely on our own understanding and desires, we limit ourselves to a perspective that is temporary and incomplete. This narrow focus often results in anxiety, frustration, and a lack of lasting peace.

The Power of a Spirit-Governed Mind

In contrast, a mind governed by the Spirit is rooted in God's truth and aligned with His purposes. The Holy Spirit transforms our thoughts, helping us to see life through the lens of faith and hope. This mindset produces peace—a deep sense of harmony with God, others, and ourselves.

A Spirit-governed mind doesn't ignore challenges or difficulties; it faces them with confidence, trusting in God's presence and promises. This peace is not passive; it actively shapes how we respond to life, empowering us to walk in faith and purpose.

Practical Steps to Develop a Spirit-Governed Mind

1. **Meditate on God's Word:**
   Regularly spend time reading and reflecting on scripture. Let His Word shape your thoughts and guide your perspective.
2. **Pray for the Holy Spirit's Guidance:**
   Invite the Holy Spirit to govern your mind each day. Ask Him to replace anxious or negative thoughts with His truth.
3. **Practice Gratitude:**
   Gratitude shifts your focus from what is lacking to what God has provided. Make a habit of thanking Him for His blessings, both big and small.
4. **Guard Your Input:**
   Be mindful of what you allow into your mind through media, conversations, and other influences. Choose content that aligns with God's truth and fosters peace.

Experiencing Life and Peace

When we allow the Spirit to govern our minds, we experience the abundant life that Jesus promised in John 10:10. This life is marked by peace, purpose, and a deep connection to God. It frees us from the burdens of worry and fear, enabling us to focus on what truly matters.

Consider the imagery of a calm river flowing through a peaceful landscape. The river's current is steady and life-giving, nourishing everything around it. In the same way, a Spirit-led mind flows with life and peace, bringing renewal and strength to every aspect of our lives.

A Testimony of a Transformed Mind

A man struggling with chronic anxiety felt trapped by his thoughts. He began meditating on Romans 8:6, praying for the Holy Spirit to govern his mind. As he immersed himself in scripture and spent time in prayer, he noticed a shift in his perspective. Worries that once consumed him began to fade, replaced by a sense of peace and trust in God. His transformation became a testimony to others, showing the power of a Spirit-led life.

Reflection on Romans 8:6

What thoughts are dominating your mind today? Write them down and place this verse beside them. Pray, "Lord, let Your Spirit govern my mind. Replace my anxious thoughts with Your peace and guide me to walk in the fullness of life You have for me."

Walking in Life and Peace

Romans 8:6 reminds us that the key to a peaceful life begins with a Spirit-governed mind. Let this verse encourage you to align your thoughts with God's truth, trusting the Holy Spirit to guide and transform you. Embrace the life and peace that come from walking in step with Him, and let His presence shape your mindset each day. With a Spirit-led mind, you can navigate life's challenges with confidence and grace.

Chapter 43: Trusting in His Plans (Jeremiah 29:11)

Verse:

"For I know the plans I have for you," declares the Lord, "plans to prosper you and not to harm you, plans to give you hope and a future."

Life's uncertainties often leave us questioning what lies ahead. Jeremiah 29:11 offers a profound assurance: God's plans for us are good. This verse reminds us that even when we don't understand the twists and turns of life, we can trust in the sovereignty and goodness of God. His plans are not just about our immediate comfort—they are about shaping us for a future filled with hope and purpose.

These words were originally spoken to the Israelites during a time of exile and uncertainty. Though their present circumstances seemed bleak, God reminded them of His long-term vision for their restoration and prosperity. This same promise applies to us today, inviting us to trust that God's plans are always for our ultimate good.

God's Knowledge of the Plan

The phrase "For I know the plans I have for you" emphasizes God's omniscience. Even when we feel lost or unsure, God knows every detail of our journey. His plans are intentional, tailored to our unique paths, and designed to lead us into His best for our lives.

Trusting in His knowledge requires surrendering our need for control. It means believing that God sees the bigger picture, even when we only see a small part of the puzzle. His perspective is eternal, guiding us toward a future that aligns with His purposes.

Plans to Prosper and Not Harm

God's plans are rooted in His love and faithfulness. The promise to prosper us and not harm us doesn't mean life will be free from challenges, but it assures us that He is always working for our good. His prosperity is not just material—it encompasses spiritual growth, relational health, and a deeper connection with Him.

This promise invites us to let go of fear and trust that God's intentions are always for our benefit. Even in seasons of waiting or difficulty, we can rest in the assurance that His plans are for our ultimate well-being.

A Future of Hope

The promise of "hope and a future" speaks to God's redemptive nature. He doesn't just sustain us in the present—He prepares us for a future filled with purpose and possibility. This hope is not wishful thinking; it is a confident expectation based on His character and promises.

When we anchor our hope in God's plans, we find peace in the midst of uncertainty. We can face the future with confidence, knowing that He is already there, guiding and providing for us every step of the way.

Practical Steps to Trust in God's Plans

1. **Surrender Your Fears:**
   Identify the areas where you struggle to trust God. Write them down and pray, asking Him to help you release control and rest in His plans.
2. **Seek His Guidance:**
   Spend time in prayer and scripture, asking God to reveal His direction for your life. Trust that He will guide you in His timing.
3. **Reflect on His Faithfulness:**
   Remember the times when God has been faithful in the past.

Let these experiences remind you of His ability to lead you through current uncertainties.

4. **Focus on the Present:**
   While trusting in His plans for the future, stay present in what God is doing today. Look for opportunities to grow, serve, and deepen your faith.

Living with Hope and Confidence

Trusting in God's plans doesn't mean life will always be easy, but it gives us the assurance that we are never alone. His plans provide a foundation of hope and a vision for the future that allows us to navigate challenges with peace and purpose.

Consider the imagery of a gardener planting seeds. The gardener knows the beauty and fruitfulness that will come, even when the seeds are buried in the soil. In the same way, God's plans for us are unfolding, even when we can't yet see the results.

A Testimony of Trusting His Plans

A young man unsure about his career felt overwhelmed by decisions and doubt. He began meditating on Jeremiah 29:11, praying for God to reveal His plans. As he trusted in God's guidance, opportunities opened that aligned with his skills and passions. Looking back, he realized how God's plans had brought him into a future filled with hope and purpose.

Reflection on Jeremiah 29:11

What areas of your life feel uncertain today? Write them down and place this verse beside them. Pray, "Lord, I trust in Your plans for my life. Help me to release my fears and walk confidently into the future You have prepared for me."

Walking in His Plans

Jeremiah 29:11 reminds us that God's plans are always for our good. Let this verse encourage you to trust in His sovereignty and love, even in the midst of uncertainty. Surrender your fears, embrace His promises, and walk forward with hope and confidence, knowing that your future is secure in His hands.

Chapter 44: The Peace of Trusting God (Proverbs 3:5-6)

Verse:

"Trust in the Lord with all your heart and lean not on your own understanding; in all your ways submit to him, and he will make your paths straight."

Trust is foundational to our relationship with God, yet it can feel challenging in moments of uncertainty. Proverbs 3:5-6 invites us to place complete trust in God, surrendering our limited understanding in favor of His infinite wisdom. This verse assures us that when we lean on Him and submit to His guidance, He will lead us down the right path.

These words, written by King Solomon, are a call to wholehearted faith. They remind us that true peace and clarity come not from relying on ourselves but from placing our confidence in the One who knows and sees all.

Wholehearted Trust

"Trust in the Lord with all your heart" emphasizes the depth of trust God desires from us. This trust is not partial or conditional—it's a total reliance on His character and promises. It means believing in His goodness even when circumstances are unclear and choosing faith over fear.

Leaning on our own understanding often leads to frustration and confusion. Our perspective is limited by what we can see and comprehend, while God's perspective is eternal and all-encompassing.

Trusting Him requires humility, acknowledging that His ways are higher than ours.

Submitting All Your Ways

Submission involves surrendering every aspect of our lives to God. This includes our plans, desires, and decisions. When we submit to Him, we align our hearts with His will, inviting Him to direct our paths.

This act of submission is not about losing control but about placing our lives in the hands of the One who loves us and knows what is best. It's an invitation to walk in step with God, trusting that His guidance will lead us to the purpose He has for us.

He Will Make Your Paths Straight

The promise of this verse is clear: when we trust and submit to God, He will make our paths straight. This doesn't mean the journey will always be easy, but it assures us that God's direction is purposeful and good. He removes obstacles, provides clarity, and leads us on the path that aligns with His perfect plan.

Practical Steps to Trust God Fully

1. **Surrender Your Plans:**
   Write down your current plans or decisions. Pray over them, asking God to align them with His will and to guide you toward the best path.
2. **Seek His Wisdom:**
   Spend time in prayer and scripture, inviting God to speak into your life. Trust that He will provide clarity in His timing.
3. **Practice Daily Submission:**
   Begin each day by committing your actions and decisions to God. Pray, "Lord, I submit this day to You. Guide me in Your

ways."

4. **Reflect on His Faithfulness:**
   Look back on times when God has guided you in the past. Let these memories strengthen your trust in His ability to lead you now.

Walking with Confidence in His Guidance

Trusting in God transforms how we navigate life's uncertainties. Instead of feeling overwhelmed or directionless, we walk with peace, knowing that He is leading us. This trust allows us to release the burden of control and rest in the assurance of His sovereignty.

Imagine walking through a dense forest with a trusted guide. You may not know the way, but your confidence in the guide allows you to move forward without fear. In the same way, trusting God gives us the courage to face the unknown, knowing that He is directing our steps.

A Testimony of Trust

A woman facing a major life decision felt paralyzed by fear of making the wrong choice. She began meditating on Proverbs 3:5-6, praying for God's guidance. As she surrendered her plans to Him, doors began to open, and she felt a clear sense of direction. Reflecting on the experience, she realized how God's guidance had brought peace and clarity to her path.

Reflection on Proverbs 3:5-6

What areas of your life feel uncertain today? Write them down and place this verse beside them. Pray, "Lord, help me to trust You with all my heart. Teach me to lean on Your wisdom and to submit my ways to You. Make my path straight and guide me in Your truth."

Walking in Trust and Peace

Proverbs 3:5-6 reminds us that trusting God leads to peace and clarity. Let this verse encourage you to place your confidence in His wisdom and guidance. Surrender your plans, seek His will, and walk forward with faith, knowing that He is leading you on the right path. With Him as your guide, you can navigate life's challenges with peace and purpose.

Chapter 45: God's Refuge in Times of Trouble (Psalm 46:1)

Verse:

"God is our refuge and strength, an ever-present help in trouble."

When life feels overwhelming, it's natural to seek a place of safety and stability. Psalm 46:1 reminds us that God Himself is our refuge and strength. This verse provides reassurance that we are never alone in our struggles—He is always present, ready to provide protection and power in our times of need.

This declaration of God's character is both comforting and empowering. It encourages us to run to Him, not just as a temporary escape but as the ultimate source of security and support. His presence transforms how we experience and respond to life's challenges.

God as Our Refuge

A refuge is a place of safety, shelter, and protection. In calling God our refuge, the psalmist emphasizes His role as a secure haven amidst life's storms. When we turn to Him, we find peace that transcends circumstances, shielding us from fear and despair.

God's refuge is not a physical location—it is His presence. This means that no matter where we are or what we face, we can find safety and rest in Him. His faithfulness ensures that His protection is unshakable, providing a foundation we can rely on.

God as Our Strength

Strength is not just about physical power—it is the inner resilience and endurance to face challenges with courage. God's strength is made perfect in our weakness, equipping us to persevere when we feel powerless. His strength renews us, giving us the ability to stand firm and move forward even in difficult times.

This strength is not something we have to muster on our own—it is a gift from God, freely available to those who seek Him. When we rely on His strength, we are empowered to face any obstacle with confidence.

An Ever-Present Help in Trouble

The phrase "ever-present help" highlights God's constancy. He is not distant or detached—He is always with us, fully aware of our needs and ready to intervene. This assurance changes how we view our struggles, reminding us that we never face them alone.

God's help is active and timely. Whether we need comfort, guidance, or provision, He meets us where we are and provides exactly what we need. His presence is a source of hope, reminding us that He is greater than any trouble we encounter.

Practical Steps to Seek Refuge in God

1. **Turn to Him First:**
   When trouble arises, resist the urge to rely solely on your own strength. Instead, turn to God in prayer, asking for His help and guidance.
2. **Meditate on His Promises:**
   Reflect on verses like Psalm 46:1 that affirm God's role as your refuge and strength. Let His Word remind you of His faithfulness.
3. **Rest in His Presence:**

Spend time in quiet reflection, focusing on God's presence. Allow His peace to calm your heart and renew your strength.

4. **Trust His Timing:**
   Remember that God's help is always timely. Trust that He is working on your behalf, even if you can't see it yet.

Living with Confidence in God's Refuge

When we trust God as our refuge and strength, we experience a peace that anchors us in the midst of life's storms. His presence gives us the courage to face challenges, knowing that He is with us and for us. This trust transforms fear into faith and uncertainty into confidence.

Consider the imagery of a fortress on a hill. No matter how fierce the storm or how strong the enemy, the fortress stands firm, protecting those within. In the same way, God is our unshakable refuge, shielding us from harm and empowering us to persevere.

A Testimony of God's Refuge

A man facing a family crisis felt overwhelmed by fear and doubt. He began meditating on Psalm 46:1, praying daily for God to be his refuge and strength. As he sought God's presence, he experienced a peace that surpassed his circumstances. Through prayer and trust, he found the courage to navigate the crisis, confident that God was his ever-present help.

Reflection on Psalm 46:1

What troubles are you facing today? Write them down and place this verse beside them. Pray, "Lord, be my refuge and strength. Help me to trust in Your presence and to find peace and power in Your protection."

Walking in God's Refuge

Psalm 46:1 reminds us that God is our ultimate source of safety and strength. Let this verse encourage you to turn to Him in times of trouble, trusting in His constant presence and unfailing help. Rest in His refuge, rely on His strength, and walk forward with the assurance that He is with you every step of the way.

Chapter 46: Courage in the Face of Fear (Joshua 1:9)

Verse:

"Have I not commanded you? Be strong and courageous. Do not be afraid; do not be discouraged, for the Lord your God will be with you wherever you go."

Fear and discouragement are natural responses to life's challenges, but Joshua 1:9 calls us to rise above them through strength and courage. These words, spoken by God to Joshua as he prepared to lead the Israelites into the Promised Land, serve as a timeless reminder that we are never alone in our battles. With God's presence, we can face anything with confidence.

This verse is both a command and a promise. It calls us to be strong and courageous, not because of our own abilities, but because of the assurance that God is with us wherever we go. His presence empowers us to overcome fear, face challenges, and move forward in faith.

A Command to Be Strong and Courageous

Strength and courage are not merely personality traits—they are choices rooted in trust and faith. To "be strong" means to stand firm in the face of adversity, while "be courageous" means to act boldly despite fear. God's command to Joshua applies to us as well, challenging us to depend on Him for the strength and courage we need.

This call is not about suppressing fear but about refusing to let it control us. It's an invitation to trust God's power and plan, even when the path ahead feels uncertain or overwhelming.

Do Not Be Afraid or Discouraged

Fear and discouragement are often rooted in uncertainty and doubt. God's command to avoid these emotions doesn't deny their reality but reminds us of His sovereignty. When we fix our eyes on Him, fear and discouragement lose their grip.

God's presence is the antidote to fear. Knowing that He is with us gives us the confidence to move forward, no matter what challenges we face. This promise assures us that we are never alone and that His power is greater than any obstacle.

For the Lord Your God Is with You

The promise "the Lord your God will be with you wherever you go" is a powerful source of comfort and encouragement. It reminds us that God's presence is not limited by time, location, or circumstance. Whether we are stepping into the unknown, facing a difficult decision, or enduring a tough season, He is always by our side.

God's presence provides guidance, strength, and peace. It assures us that we are not walking alone but are accompanied by the One who holds all things together.

Practical Steps to Cultivate Strength and Courage

1. **Anchor Yourself in God's Word:**
   Meditate on scriptures like Joshua 1:9 that affirm God's presence and power. Let His Word strengthen your faith and resolve.
2. **Pray for Boldness:**
   Ask God to give you the courage to face your fears and the strength to persevere. Trust that He will equip you for every challenge.
3. **Focus on His Presence:**

When fear or discouragement arises, remind yourself that God is with you. Take a moment to pray and acknowledge His presence.

4. **Take Small Steps of Faith:**
   Courage often grows with action. Start by taking small, faithful steps toward the challenges before you, trusting God to guide you.

Living with Courage and Confidence

When we embrace God's command to be strong and courageous, we experience a peace that transcends fear. His presence empowers us to face challenges with confidence, knowing that He is working for our good. This courage doesn't come from within—it is a gift from God, fueled by His Spirit and promises.

Imagine a child learning to ride a bike, hesitant and unsure. But with a parent's steady hand and encouraging words, the child finds the courage to pedal forward. In the same way, God's presence steadies and strengthens us, helping us move forward with confidence and faith.

A Testimony of Strength and Courage

A young woman facing a career transition felt paralyzed by fear of failure. She began meditating on Joshua 1:9, praying for God to give her courage and strength. As she trusted in His presence, she took small steps toward her goals. Each step built her confidence, and she eventually found herself in a position that exceeded her expectations, a testament to God's faithfulness.

Reflection on Joshua 1:9

What fears or challenges are you facing today? Write them down and place this verse beside them. Pray, "Lord, help me to be strong and courageous. Remind me of Your presence and give me the confidence to trust in Your plan."

Walking in Strength and Courage

Joshua 1:9 reminds us that God's presence is the source of our strength and courage. Let this verse encourage you to face life's challenges with faith, trusting in His guidance and provision. Be strong, be courageous, and walk forward with the assurance that God is with you wherever you go.

Chapter 47: The Power of Gratitude (1 Thessalonians 5:18)

Verse:

"Give thanks in all circumstances; for this is God's will for you in Christ Jesus."

Gratitude is a powerful force that shifts our focus from what is lacking to what is present. In 1 Thessalonians 5:18, Paul instructs us to give thanks in all circumstances. This doesn't mean we are thankful for every difficulty, but rather, we recognize God's presence and provision regardless of the situation. Gratitude aligns our hearts with God's will, helping us to see life through the lens of His grace.

This verse challenges us to adopt an attitude of thankfulness, even in the midst of challenges. It invites us to trust that God is working for our good and to express our faith through gratitude, which brings peace and joy to our lives.

Giving Thanks in All Circumstances

Life is full of highs and lows, moments of joy and seasons of struggle. Paul's command to give thanks in all circumstances is a call to recognize God's sovereignty and goodness, even when things don't go as planned. Gratitude in difficult times doesn't deny the reality of pain—it acknowledges that God's love and faithfulness remain constant.

This perspective shifts our focus from the problem to the Provider. It reminds us that no matter what we face, God is with us, offering His strength, guidance, and comfort.

God's Will for Us

Gratitude is not just a suggestion—it is God's will for us in Christ Jesus. Living with a thankful heart reflects our trust in Him and our recognition of His blessings. When we cultivate gratitude, we align ourselves with His purposes and open our hearts to experience His peace and joy.

This attitude of thankfulness transforms how we approach life. It deepens our faith, strengthens our relationships, and equips us to face challenges with resilience and hope.

Practical Steps to Cultivate Gratitude

1. **Start a Gratitude Journal:**
   Each day, write down three things you are thankful for. This practice helps you focus on God's blessings and shifts your perspective.
2. **Pray with Thanksgiving:**
   Begin your prayers with gratitude. Thank God for His provision, protection, and presence in your life.
3. **Express Thanks to Others:**
   Take time to thank the people in your life who have supported or encouraged you. Gratitude fosters stronger connections and uplifts those around you.
4. **Look for Blessings in Challenges:**
   When facing difficulties, ask God to show you His presence and purpose in the situation. Trust that He is working for your good.

Living a Life of Gratitude

A life of gratitude is not free from challenges, but it is marked by peace and joy. When we focus on God's goodness, we find the strength to navigate difficulties with faith and resilience. Gratitude transforms our hearts, reminding us that God's blessings are abundant, even in the midst of trials.

Consider the imagery of a sunrise after a storm. The clouds may linger, but the light breaks through, illuminating the beauty of the world. In the same way, gratitude allows us to see God's light in the midst of life's storms, bringing hope and renewal to our hearts.

A Testimony of Gratitude

A man recovering from a serious illness felt overwhelmed by his limitations. He began practicing daily gratitude, focusing on small blessings like the support of loved ones and moments of progress. As he cultivated thankfulness, his perspective shifted. He found joy in the journey of recovery and saw how God's grace had carried him through.

Reflection on 1 Thessalonians 5:18

What are you thankful for today? Write down three things and place this verse beside them. Pray, "Lord, thank You for Your constant presence and provision. Help me to give thanks in all circumstances and to trust in Your plan for my life."

Walking in Gratitude

1 Thessalonians 5:18 reminds us that gratitude is an essential part of our faith. Let this verse encourage you to embrace thankfulness, even in challenging times. Focus on God's blessings, express your gratitude, and trust in His faithfulness. With a heart of thankfulness, you can face every season with peace, joy, and confidence.

Chapter 48: God's Strength in Every Challenge (Philippians 4:13)

Verse:

"I can do all things through Christ who strengthens me."

Life often presents us with challenges that test our endurance, courage, and faith. Philippians 4:13 is a powerful reminder that we are not alone in these moments. Through Christ, we have access to a strength that enables us to face anything life throws our way. This verse is not just about accomplishing great feats but about trusting in God's power to sustain us in every situation.

Paul wrote these words while imprisoned, highlighting that the strength he speaks of is not dependent on external circumstances but on his reliance on Christ. This strength is not our own—it comes from the One who empowers us, equipping us to endure, overcome, and thrive.

What It Means to Do All Things Through Christ

The "all things" Paul refers to encompasses every aspect of life, from enduring hardships to fulfilling God's calling. This verse doesn't mean we can achieve anything we desire, but it assures us that Christ's strength is sufficient for whatever He has called us to do.

This strength is not just about physical or mental stamina—it is a deep, inner resilience that comes from the Holy Spirit. It empowers us to face challenges with confidence, persevere through difficulties, and live out our faith boldly.

Strength Beyond Our Own

Relying on our own strength often leads to frustration and burnout. But when we depend on Christ, we tap into a limitless source of power. His strength is made perfect in our weakness, enabling us to do what we could never accomplish on our own.

This truth encourages us to let go of self-reliance and embrace God's sufficiency. It reminds us that our limitations are opportunities for His strength to shine through.

Practical Steps to Rely on Christ's Strength

1. **Pray for His Empowerment:**
   Begin each day by asking Christ to strengthen you for the challenges ahead. Trust that His power is enough to sustain you.
2. **Meditate on His Promises:**
   Reflect on scriptures like Philippians 4:13 that affirm Christ's strength in your life. Let His Word renew your confidence.
3. **Take One Step at a Time:**
   When faced with a daunting challenge, focus on taking small, faithful steps. Trust that Christ will provide the strength you need for each moment.
4. **Celebrate His Power at Work:**
   Recognize and thank God for the ways He strengthens and sustains you. Gratitude deepens your trust in His provision.

Facing Challenges with Confidence

When we rely on Christ's strength, we can face life's challenges with peace and confidence. His power equips us to endure trials, overcome obstacles, and fulfill His purposes. This reliance transforms how we approach difficulties, shifting our focus from our limitations to His limitless power.

Consider the imagery of a vine and its branches. The branches cannot bear fruit on their own—they must remain connected to the vine for sustenance and strength. In the same way, we must remain connected to Christ, drawing from His power to thrive and grow.

A Testimony of Christ's Strength

A woman juggling a demanding job and family responsibilities felt overwhelmed by the weight of her obligations. She began meditating on Philippians 4:13, praying daily for Christ's strength. As she trusted in His power, she found the energy and peace to navigate her challenges. Her reliance on Christ became a source of inspiration to those around her, showing the transformative power of His strength.

Reflection on Philippians 4:13

What challenges are you facing today that feel insurmountable? Write them down and place this verse beside them. Pray, "Lord, I trust in Your strength. Equip me to face these challenges and to walk in the power of Your Spirit."

Walking in His Strength

Philippians 4:13 reminds us that we can face any challenge through Christ's strength. Let this verse encourage you to rely on Him in every situation, trusting in His power to sustain and equip you. No matter what you face, walk forward with confidence, knowing that His strength is sufficient for every moment.

Chapter 49: Walking by Faith, Not by Sight (2 Corinthians 5:7)

Verse:

"For we live by faith, not by sight."

Life often requires us to navigate the unknown, making decisions and taking steps without fully understanding where the path will lead. 2 Corinthians 5:7 reminds us that as believers, we are called to walk by faith, trusting in God's promises rather than relying solely on what we can see. This verse is a powerful encouragement to place our confidence in God, even when the journey ahead feels uncertain.

Faith is not about denying reality—it's about trusting in a greater reality: God's sovereignty and goodness. When we walk by faith, we acknowledge that His perspective is far greater than ours, and we choose to rely on Him rather than our limited understanding.

The Meaning of Living by Faith

Living by faith involves trusting in God's character, promises, and guidance, even when we can't see the full picture. It requires surrendering our need for control and stepping forward with confidence that He is leading us.

Faith is not a passive belief; it's an active trust. It's about moving forward in obedience to God, even when we don't have all the answers. This trust grows as we experience His faithfulness and learn to rely on Him in every aspect of our lives.

Not By Sight

Walking by sight means relying on what is visible and tangible, often leading to fear and hesitation when the path ahead is unclear. Walking by faith, however, means trusting in God's unseen hand, knowing that He is working behind the scenes for our good.

This doesn't mean we ignore challenges or difficulties—it means we choose to focus on God's promises rather than our circumstances. Faith allows us to move forward with hope, even when the way forward feels uncertain.

Practical Steps to Walk by Faith

1. **Trust His Word:**
   Spend time in scripture, letting God's promises shape your perspective. His Word is a lamp to your feet and a light to your path (Psalm 119:105).
2. **Pray for Guidance:**
   Seek God's direction in your decisions and steps. Trust that He will guide you in His perfect timing.
3. **Take Faithful Action:**
   Faith requires movement. Take small steps in obedience to God's leading, trusting that He will provide what you need along the way.
4. **Celebrate His Faithfulness:**
   Reflect on how God has been faithful in the past. Let these memories strengthen your trust in His guidance for the future.

Faith Over Fear

Walking by faith doesn't eliminate fear, but it empowers us to overcome it. When we trust in God's presence and promises, fear loses its grip. This trust allows us to navigate the unknown with confidence, knowing that He is with us every step of the way.

Consider the imagery of a hiker following a guide through a dense forest. The hiker may not see the path ahead, but they trust the guide to lead them safely. In the same way, our faith in God enables us to move forward, trusting Him to direct our steps.

A Testimony of Faith

A man faced with a career opportunity felt overwhelmed by uncertainty about whether to take the leap. He began meditating on 2 Corinthians 5:7, praying for the faith to trust God's guidance. As he stepped forward in obedience, doors opened, and he experienced God's provision in ways he hadn't expected. Looking back, he realized that walking by faith had led him to a season of growth and blessing.

Reflection on 2 Corinthians 5:7

What areas of your life require you to walk by faith today? Write them down and place this verse beside them. Pray, "Lord, help me to trust in Your guidance and to walk by faith, not by sight. Strengthen my confidence in Your promises."

Walking by Faith

2 Corinthians 5:7 reminds us that faith is essential to our journey with God. Let this verse encourage you to trust in His promises, even when the path ahead feels unclear. Walk by faith, leaning on His guidance and trusting in His presence. With Him as your guide, you can face every step with confidence and peace.

Chapter 50: God's Promise of Rest (Matthew 11:28)

Verse:

"Come to me, all you who are weary and burdened, and I will give you rest."

The burdens of life can feel overwhelming, leaving us tired, anxious, and in need of relief. Matthew 11:28 is a heartfelt invitation from Jesus to bring our weariness and burdens to Him. He doesn't promise to eliminate every challenge, but He assures us that in Him, we will find rest for our souls.

This verse is not only a call to find relief but a reminder that true rest is found in the presence of Christ. It is an offer of peace, renewal, and hope for those who feel weighed down by the demands of life.

Come to Me

The invitation "Come to me" emphasizes the personal nature of Jesus' call. He doesn't point us to a formula or a process—He points us to Himself. Coming to Jesus means turning to Him in faith, trusting that He can provide what we need.

This act of coming requires humility. It means acknowledging our limitations and recognizing that we cannot carry life's burdens on our own. It's an act of surrender, choosing to trust Jesus over our own strength.

All Who Are Weary and Burdened

Jesus' invitation is open to everyone, but it is especially for those who feel the weight of life's challenges. Weariness can come from physical exhaustion, emotional strain, or spiritual struggles. Whatever form it takes, Jesus sees and understands our burdens.

Being burdened often means carrying responsibilities, worries, or pain that feel too heavy to bear. Jesus doesn't dismiss these struggles—He invites us to bring them to Him, knowing that He can provide the relief we need.

I Will Give You Rest

The promise of rest is both immediate and eternal. In the present, Jesus offers peace that calms our hearts and renews our strength. This rest doesn't mean an absence of challenges but a deep assurance that we are held and sustained by His love.

Eternal rest points to the ultimate peace we will experience in His presence forever. It's the promise of a life free from pain, striving, and sorrow—a hope that anchors us even in the midst of life's difficulties.

Practical Steps to Find Rest in Christ

1. **Bring Your Burdens to Him:**
   In prayer, name the specific burdens you're carrying. Lay them at Jesus' feet, trusting Him to provide relief and guidance.
2. **Spend Time in His Presence:**
   Rest begins with connection. Spend time reading scripture, worshiping, or simply sitting in silence with God, allowing His presence to refresh you.
3. **Practice Sabbath Rest:**
   Set aside regular time to rest from work and focus on God. Use this time to recharge physically, emotionally, and

spiritually.

4. **Trust His Timing:**
   Rest doesn't always come immediately. Trust that Jesus is working in your life, even when you don't see immediate results.

Living in His Rest

Living in the rest Jesus offers doesn't mean life will always be easy, but it transforms how we experience our challenges. His rest equips us to face life with peace, strength, and hope, knowing that we are not alone.

Consider the imagery of a shepherd leading his sheep to a quiet pasture. The sheep rest, trusting the shepherd's care and provision. In the same way, Jesus leads us to places of rest and renewal, providing for our needs and restoring our souls.

A Testimony of Rest

A woman overwhelmed by the demands of caregiving and work felt like she had nothing left to give. She began meditating on Matthew 11:28, praying for Jesus to provide rest for her weary soul. As she spent time in His presence, she found peace and renewal. Though her circumstances didn't change immediately, her heart was refreshed, and she experienced the sustaining power of His rest.

Reflection on Matthew 11:28

What burdens are you carrying today? Write them down and place this verse beside them. Pray, "Lord, I come to You with my weariness and burdens. Help me to trust in Your promise of rest and to find renewal in Your presence."

Walking in His Rest

Matthew 11:28 is a beautiful reminder that Jesus is the source of true rest. Let this verse encourage you to bring your burdens to Him, trusting in His love and care. Rest in His presence, draw strength from His promises, and move forward with the assurance that His peace will sustain you through every season.

Carrying Peace Into Tomorrow

As you close this book, take a moment to reflect on the journey you've undertaken. You've explored God's promises, uncovered tools to manage stress and anxiety, and embraced His peace. This is not the end—it's the beginning of a life filled with greater trust and deeper faith.

Stress and anxiety may not disappear overnight, but they no longer have to define you. Through the scriptures we've explored, you've seen that God's peace is always available. It's not something you have to earn; it's a gift, waiting for you to receive it. Each day, God invites you to surrender your burdens, trust in His plan, and walk forward with confidence in His love.

Remember, peace isn't about avoiding challenges. It's about finding assurance in God's presence, even in life's storms. The world may tell you to carry it all on your own, but God's Word reminds you that you don't have to. Lean into His strength and let Him carry what feels too heavy.

The lessons in this book are tools to keep with you: prayer as your refuge, gratitude as your shield, and trust as your foundation. When anxiety creeps in, return to the scriptures that spoke to your heart. Meditate on their truths and let them anchor you in God's unchanging promises.

Take practical steps to live this peace daily. Pray honestly, thank God for what you have, and trust Him with what's uncertain. These habits will transform how you approach stress and anxiety, making God's peace a constant companion in your life.

As you move forward, embrace the truth that you are never alone. God walks beside you, guarding your heart and strengthening your spirit. Whatever tomorrow brings, face it with courage and faith. Let these scriptures be a light to guide your path and a reminder that God's peace is yours to carry.

Step boldly into the life God has for you—with faith over fear and a heart anchored in His promises.

About The Author

Willie London II

Willie London II is a writer, educator, and passionate advocate for faith-based personal growth. With a Bachelor's degree in English from Southeastern Louisiana University and years of experience as a teacher and behavioral health professional, Willie combines his love for storytelling and teaching to inspire others.

Having spent years studying scripture and cultivating his own relationship with Christ, Willie understands the challenges of managing stress and anxiety in a demanding world. His mission is to make faith accessible and relatable, helping others discover peace and purpose through God's Word.

In addition to his work as an author, Willie is a creator, entrepreneur, and motivator, sharing insights on TikTok and other platforms to encourage others to step into their God-given potential. He believes in the power of scripture to transform lives and hopes this book will be a tool for readers to find strength, rest, and renewal in Christ.

www.ingramcontent.com/pod-product-compliance
Lightning Source LLC
LaVergne TN
LVHW041030150826
845672LV00001B/247
* 9 7 9 8 2 3 0 0 2 3 3 4 0 *